Growing Up In Bay City Oregon

Growing Up In Bay City Oregon

A Memoir
1936 - 1953

Gordon Lee

CALIBER PRESS

Spanaway, WA
Caliber-Press.com

Caliber Press
P.O. Box 4162
Spanaway, WA
www.caliberpress.com
kim@caliber-press.com

ISBN: 978-1-7372908-1-0

Library of Congress Cataloging-in-Publication Data:

2021910440

Author Disclaimer: I have tried to recreate events, locales and conversations from my memories of them. In order to maintain their anonymity in some instances I have changed the names of individuals.

Front Cover, Book Design, & Editing by Kimberly Swetland
Cover Photography by Kimberly Swetland
Author Photograph by Gary Swetland

Printed in the United States of America
Paperback Edition / July 2021
First Edition

10 9 8 7 6 5 4 3 2 1

Dedicated To My Mother.

Dorothy Maxine Pratt
1913 - 1990
1937 photograph of my mother, age 24, holding me at age one.

Table of Contents

Preface

I wrote this book to preserve my family history and facts. I've never discussed some of these things with my family members. My worry is that most of a family's history dies when the older family members pass on. Now that I'm 84, I wanted to pass on what facts I can remember. I do not intend this book to make anyone feel sorry for me as a child growing up.

The Great Depression and WW2 caused a lot of my hardships during this period of my life. It taught me to "make do," which was a phrase used by poor families during and following the Depression and WW2. It meant to get by with what you have, when you have very little or nothing at all.

Having grown up with all my hardships, I would not trade my childhood for anything different. I made things happen for me. I have done many things other people only dream about doing.

By Gordon Lee
DOB 08-5-1936

Part I
My Life Before Bay City
1936 ~ 1945

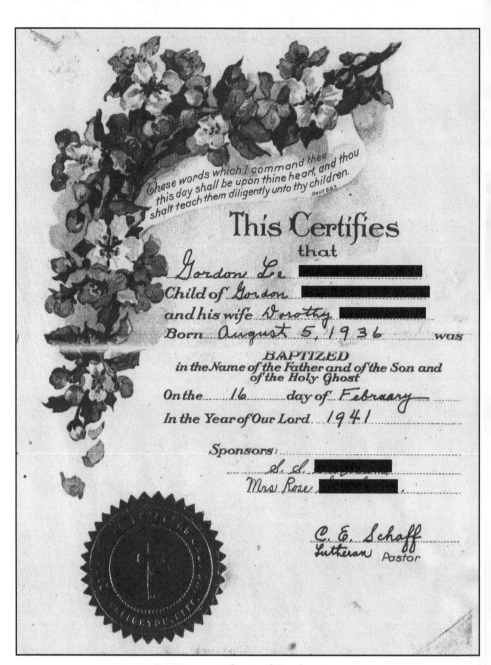

These words which I command thee this day shall be upon thine heart, and thou shalt teach them diligently unto thy children.
Deut. 6.6,7.

This Certifies
that

Gordon Le ▬▬▬▬

Child of *Gordon* ▬▬▬▬

and his wife *Dorothy* ▬▬▬▬

Born *August 5, 1936* was

BAPTIZED
in the Name of the Father and of the Son and of the Holy Ghost

On the ___16___ day of *February*

In the Year of Our Lord ___*1941*___

Sponsors:

S. S. ▬▬▬▬

Mrs Rose ▬▬▬▬

C. E. Schaff
Lutheran Pastor

Baptism certificate of Gordon Lee.

Nebraska
1936 - 1942

Omaha, Nebraska

I was born in 1936 during the Great Depression in Omaha, Nebraska where my dad worked for Watson Brothers Long Haul Trucking and my mother worked as a nurse's aide in the hospital where I was born. Dad was a dock foreman and load dispatcher. He was just discharged from the US Army, where he was First Cornet in the Army band. Dad and five Army friends worked nights in the bars playing music and stayed at a club as long as the tip jar was fed. He earned enough doing night work to buy a new 1937 Ford Coupe. His band traveled from club to club in an eight-passenger Packard car with two jump seats. Their tip jar that sat on the piano was a cat whose head moved from side to side. Dad drove the Ford when we left Nebraska, going to Oregon in 1942. Later, he traded it in for a 1950 Chevrolet 2 door.

The economy was so bad for us in Nebraska, that, for example, my mom's icebox was an orange crate nailed to the outside wall of the kitchen by a window. Mom had to open the window and reach outside to get milk from the box. We could not use this makeshift icebox in the summer. In 1936, many U.S. cities and homes weren't yet wired for electricity. Most folks had ice boxes and purchased ice from the ice delivery man or stores at 1 cent to 5 cents per lb. We lived in Council Bluffs, Iowa, just across the Missouri River, which was the scene of councils with Indians and Lewis and Clark. Council Bluffs was a short drive to the east, from Omaha City Center.

Gordon Sr. (Right) and friend (Left), Norfolk, 1930.

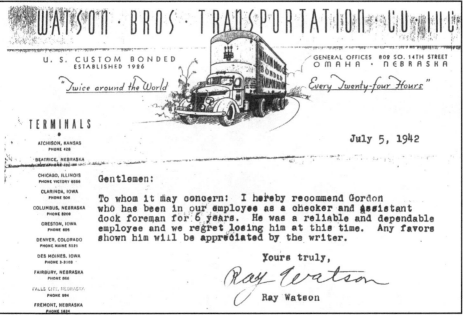

A letter of recommendation Dad received from his employment at Watson.

Gordon, Dorothy, and Gordon Lee in Omaha, 3 March 1936.

Cedar Bluff Farm, Verdigris Township, Antelope County, Nebraska.

The Township of Verdigris, Nebraska

On July 24, 1938, my brother Billy Joe was born and because of the Depression, my parents took me to my grandparents' 293-acre homestead farm to live in the township of Verdigris, Nebraska in the northern part of Antelope County. My fathers' mom and dad took good care of me and assigned my dad's brother Lee, who still lived on the farm at age 23, to look after me. He had to feed me, bathe me, and change my diapers. After I left the farm in 1942, Uncle Lee joined the Army as a medic. Uncle Lee and I were very close. He wrote me letters during the war and also sent me a French banknote that I still own. Uncle Lee was in Europe for several months, caring for wounded troops on the front line.

Later on, when I was six, I was still too young to know the details about the 10" x 12" red, white, and blue flag with a blue 3 inch star in the center displayed in our living room window facing the city street for people passing by our house to see. On the lower white background of the flag, made of a sturdy burlap material, were the words, 'IN THE SERVICE.' Many families proudly displayed these flags. We displayed one in honor of my uncle Lee, who was sent to Europe as a medic during WWII. While looking at those flags on display in various houses you did not want to see a flag with a gold star in the center because that meant their family member died in the war. I framed the flag that was on display when we lived in our house in Portland, Oregon and it is now hanging on the wall in my dining room. My mom had given the flag to me while I was in the USMC after my 18-month tour of duty in Hawaii.

The farm near Creighton, Nebraska, was well over 100 miles from where my parents lived. My Grandpa Sam was very respected by all and had positions with the county over the years as county tax assessor and county road commissioner. All the county roads were gravel at the time. Grandpa assigned my dad and Lee to grade roads using a large scoop pan with handlebars, pulled by a team of draft horses. One time, Uncle Lee broke his leg operating the scoop while trying to get rid of some potholes.

Grandpa also leased about 2,000 acres to farm. He raised chickens, pigs, horses, and other livestock along with miles of corn and hay. The farmhouse is still lived in by someone and stands on a small hill facing the gravel road. Grandpa had a large barn and other outbuildings with a very large crab apple tree from which he made cider. Grandma Rose was a school teacher but had

Gordon Lee's Uncle Lee.

French bank note from Uncle Lee.

Samuel on Prince, holding Gordon Lee on the farm, 1930s.

Gordon Lee's Grandma, Rose Hehn, late 1930s.

to resign when she married. Back then female teachers weren't allowed to be married. Marriage restricted the employment of women in certain occupations, such as teaching and some clerical positions.

All grandma's kids were born at home. Doctors made house calls back then and delivered babies. A doctor with the last name Gordon delivered my dad and grandma named him after Dr. Gordon. Since Grandma was a state-certified teacher, she homeschooled all of her children. She was a Lutheran and took me to church every Sunday and had me baptized in the Creighton Lutheran Church. Despite her passion for religion, I never understood how my dad was an Atheist and told me repeatedly there wasn't a God, while I was growing up.

During the winter months, the snow was higher than the windows on the first floor of the house, so one had to go up to the second floor to see outside. The snowbank at the roadside was so high you couldn't see vehicles going down the road. The house had a covered shed-like walkway leading from the house to the barn in the winter because of the deep snow. At night, Grandma would heat bricks in her wood stove oven, wrap them in cloth and put them under my feet in bed.

We had fried chicken one or two times a week. Grandma would grab a chicken, kill it using an ax and chopping block in the backyard near the back door, then pluck its feathers. Grandma always put the neck bone on my plate, knowing it was my favorite.

Grandma and Grandpa's house sat up on a small hill about a city block above the county gravel road. To purchase postal supplies like stamps and postcards, postal customers left a note for the postman along with cash in their mailboxes, and he filled their order and left change. I can only imagine what would happen if people left cash in their mailboxes today. This practice of mailmen selling postal supplies saved the farmers a lot of time and trips to the cities. When grandma was expecting a package or other mail that she was in a hurry to get, rather than walk the city block to the mailbox she could address a postcard to herself to see if she had mail. She'd put it in her mailbox lifting the red flag on the box and look out her living room window from time to time. When the red flag was down, the mailman had been there. The pre-stamped postcards cost one cent each.

My grandpa, dad, and Uncle Lee were very musically inclined. My dad played over eight instruments, which included the organ, piano, banjo, guitar, cornet, trumpet, and others. On Saturday nights, while dad was growing up, grandpa drove to Yangton, South Dakota with dad and Lee to play music on their own radio show. Yangton was as well known for music, at the time, as Nashville is today. Mel Tillis and Lawrence Welk had radio shows at the same radio station. Later in life while in Branson, Missouri, dad introduced me to Mel Tillis, and we had a nice visit.

My dad made pocket money by collecting the bounty placed on crows because they overran the county. Dad used his shotgun to kill the crows. Shotgun shells cost $.05 cents each, back then, and the bounty paid by the county was $.25 cents per bird. Of course, Dad would often try to get more than one bird per shot. The county paid an employee to sit at a small table, placed on a downtown city sidewalk in Creighton, who counted the dead birds and paid the bounty with cash. Counting the dead birds without handling them was easy, as the county required that the bird's heads were kept and placed in a glass jar with the lid on. After receiving his bounty, Dad bought shells to replace those he had used and what money he had left was his profit. The county set up a bounty table every Saturday, weather permitting.

In the meantime, the Government kept after Dad to get a war effort job or he would get drafted back into the Army even though he had already served, was married with kids, and had employment. In early 1942 we moved to Oregon to avoid the Army draft and so my father could get a war effort job. My mom, dad, and younger brother Billy came to the farm to pick me up for the drive to the West Coast. Initially, their plan was to check out Seattle for a job for dad and a place to live. Seattle did not feel right for dad so we went South to Oregon. When my family arrived at the farm, Grandpa came riding up on his horse, wearing his gun belt and his .45 revolver. He also had his new white Stetson cowboy hat on. His horse had one of the best saddles ever made. It was a Miles City Montana, which were expensive. Grandpa dismounted and, feeling playful, he tossed his new cowboy hat about twenty feet across the lawn, handed the revolver to mom and said, "I will bet you can't hit the hat." Mom shot five times and put two holes into grandpa's new hat. My mom smiled and said, "I have never shot a gun before."

The four of us fit into the 1937 Ford Coupe with only a front bench seat. Billy and I rode on the panel under the rear window. Our car trunk was full of kitchen items and clothing. I only remember seeing my parents two other times while I lived with my grandparents, which was for about four years. In 1942, when we traveled to Oregon to start a new life, I barely knew them.

On our way West, in the middle of nowhere in Eastern Oregon, we saw several signs that read, 'Stop Ahead and See the Rattlers'. We came to a gravel vehicle turn-out beside the two-lane highway and Dad pulled over. There were signs near the pullout and near a big hole in the ground was another sign that read, 'Beware of Rattlers'. A short dirt path led to the hole with more signage that read, 'Look Out For Rattleshakes'. My mom was afraid of anything involving risk, but saw the writing on the wall: both of her boys wanted to see the rattlers. My brother and I kept a tight hold on her hands and peered over the railing. The hole was filled with baby rattles.

Dorothy on the way to Oregon, 1942.

Gordon, Gordon Lee, and Billie, 1940.

Dorothy and Billie, 1940.

Milwaukie, Oregon
1942

Our trip West ended in Milwaukie, Oregon, a short distance South of Portland City Center. First, Dad gained employment at the Oregon City Paper Mill, which wasn't hard to do, as most men were now in the military. Dad had 50 cents left and bought two quarts of milk for my brother and me. We didn't have anywhere to live so Dad stopped at a row of log cabins and talked to the female manager who agreed to let us stay in a cabin and pay her out of Dad's first paycheck, which was not uncommon, as most people trusted one another then. There were pots, pans and a large box of food left over after our trip West.

Mom visited our neighbor lady in the cabin beside ours. She learned single ladies lived in all the other cabins, and it was a prostitution business. Mom felt embarrassed and became furious. She made Dad agree to move out on his next payday.

While we lived there, I made a friend who owned a bike and agreed to give me a ride on the handlebars. My foot came into contact with the front wheel spokes, and they ripped the heel of my shoe off. Because we moved out of the cabins we didn't have anywhere to stay. Dad was forced to quit his job in the paper mill when the government said it did not qualify as a war effort job, but to make matters worse, I didn't have any shoes.

Portland, Oregon
1942

We drove to Portland and Dad got a war effort job as a welder at the Kaiser Shipyard on Swan Island building warships. The Kaiser Company also made automobiles.

I entered Woodstock Grade School as a first grader in 1942. I only lived with my dad I was one and two years old, so knew little about him. Dad worked midnight to 8 a.m. and slept days. After getting up around 5 p.m., he ate dinner. Then he went to the driveway to sit in the car, listen to music and drink whiskey. Dad worked seven days a week at the shipyard and saved enough money for a down payment on the house we lived in on S.E. Cooper Street. The property had several Queen Ann cherry trees and one large Bing cherry tree about 60 feet tall.

We would pick the cherries and my mom put them in canning jars to store in our cellar under the house. When my brother or I wanted a snack, they fit the bill. Mom would can about 5 dozen or more jars of cherries at a time and they kept for a long time in the dark, damp cellar.

My possessions were very limited. When we lived in Portland, all of my clothing came from a Goodwill store. I slept on a Goodwill canvas cot with wooden side rails that hurt my arm if I hit them on the wood during the night. In all my years living at home never slept on sheets. Instead, I slept between two Army wool surplus blankets purchased from Goodwill. My parents never bought me toys or threw me a birthday part when I was a kid. The best birthday I had was when my friend 'Puddy' and his mother came over to my house and gave me a quarter and a banana. In the years living at home, I never got a dime allowance. I made my own money.

During the years I lived in Portland, we only left the house as a family four or five times. One time we went to a grocery store on 82nd Street, one

Aerial of Swan Island Shipyards.
Courtesy Oregon Hist. Soc. Researc Lib., Orhi49686

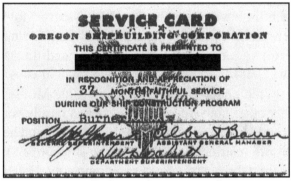

Dad's shipyard service card.

Shipyard Award presented to my dad in 1945.

time to Oaks Park (an amusement park), but we only watched other people there for a short amount of time and left. We went to one Rose Parade in June of 1944, at which time we passed by The Blue Mouse Movie House which displayed large neon blue mice on the exterior of the building that advertised that they showed two kids movies, two cartoons and the Movietone News (WWII war news), all for 35 cents every Saturday. I always wanted to go to this movie house, but never did. Just the name Blue Mouse was a come on for kids. The only other time we left the house as a family was when dad had a large pile of weeds, brush and tree limbs to get rid of and he could not burn them because of fire restrictions so he rented a small, open bed trailer so he could haul the yard debris across town to a dump area. Dad towed the trailer with our 1937 Ford. He stopped for a red light and we heard a loud thud and saw our trailer wheel pass our car on the left side. It traveled through the intersection and came to rest on the front of a business. Dad inspected the trailer and discovered it only had one lug nut holding the wheel on and it gave out when dad made his stop at the red light. We never ate out at a restaurant while I lived in Portland. As a matter of fact, I never ate out with mom or dad until I was out of the USMC in October 1956. During the first 23 years of my life there were no fast-food restaurants.

While walking on Cooper Street when I was nine years old and my brother was seven, we were stopped by a man in a car who offered us a job as paperboys delivering the Portland Shopping News once per week. The man delivered about 100 papers to us after taking us in his car to show us our route, which was about one-half mile from our house. At our age, we could not remember where to deliver after he showed us one time, so we just took the papers and left them in piles on a wooded lot. That job lasted two weeks with no pay.

I picked cherries from our trees and sold them in small boxes door to door for over a month every year. I always sold them all. Our neighbor, Mr. Dickson, had a garden a city block long and several feet wide. I picked his produce during the non-cherry season and sold it door to door. Mr. Dickson paid my dad a visit and showed him where produce was missing from his garden. Soon after that I went to the garden, got down on my hands and knees, and ate the tops off of several cabbages. From then on, Mr. Dickson and Dad agreed rabbits were taking the produce.

At age 10, I knocked on doors asking for a job. One nice older lady had me climb up into her loft to clean and put everything in order. She paid me

$5 for the day's work. I also went door to door, picking up newspapers and tin cans for the war effort. The tin cans had to have the paper labels torn off, both ends cut out, and they had to be smashed flat. I delivered them to Wood-stock School gym, which was stacked full of cans at times, so it couldn't be used for school activities.

On a Sunday afternoon, an old Italian lady came into our yard crying and yelling, "you killed my geese." She had the geese in each hand, swinging them around. Dad went to the yard to see what all the commotion was about. Apparently, my younger brother had gone to the lady's yard, that was two blocks from our house, entered her chicken and geese pen and killed four geese using a stick. The lady was yelling in English and in Italian. Dad must have paid the lady for her loss because she left our yard with the dead geese. Dad headed for the house, and my brother headed for our bedroom.

My mother was housebound and didn't know how to drive a car. To my knowledge, she only left the house on Sundays when Dad took the family on about a 2-hour drive. The only other time she left the house was for emergencies, such as my brother's appendix operation. But there was one occasion when both she and Dad went somewhere during the night and left us kids home alone. We were very young and scared. We hid under the table and stayed there until they returned.

Having nothing, you learned how to 'make do'–a Depression Era and WWII saying. Thinking back, maybe I was better off later in life for it, except for the toll it took on my teeth and body for not owning a toothbrush and lack of good quality food. When not in school, we found plenty of things to do that cost little or nothing.

An open field about a city block long and a block wide sat across the street from our house. We learned about foxholes during WWII, so we dug a large 'command' fox hole 10 feet long, 3 feet wide, and 3 feet deep with dirt from the hole used as a barrier around the hole. My friend who was in my grade at school also dug a hole on the far side of the field behind his house. We dug little holes on the inside of our hole to hold or hide things, including rocks. Puddy and a couple of other boys engaged in rock fights with my brother and me. Our fox holes were too far apart for us to hit one another, but on a good day, about 50 rocks went flying in either direction.

We also had fun going to another friend's property that we called Eddie's Woods about three blocks from our house. The woods were filled with 15 to 20-foot-tall Alder and Vine Maple trees. We spent hours climbing trees, We also had fun going to another friend's property that we called Eddie's Woods about three blocks from our house. 15 to 20-foot-tall Alder and Vine Maple trees filled the woods. We spent hours climbing trees, sometimes holding on to the top of a tree and then jumping to the ground.

We would also spend hours at the freight yard train tracks. The trains would slow down to 5 to 10 miles per hour while traveling on the multi-tracks about a mile from our house. We could run and catch a boxcar, holding onto its ladder and ride for a mile or so, then catch another boxcar going the other direction to return to our starting point. Sometimes hobos also rode the trains. One time a bum riding in a boxcar half full of watermelons tossed a melon to us as he went by.

Having a watermelon but no knife to cut it open was a problem. I hit the melon on the railroad tracks several times to open it up. The pieces of watermelon weren't pretty, but we thought they tasted very good. After eating all the watermelon we could, we found an old empty pork and beans can a bum had discarded and had a seed spitting contest into the can. This proved too difficult, so we drew lines in the dirt beside the railroad tracks and spat seeds for distance.

Another trip to the railroad tracks yielded us a windfall. We found several explosive caps used by railroad work crews to alert the train engineer the tracks were being worked on ahead. A train would run over these caps attached by two wires to the track and they would explode. The cap had glue and sand on the bottom so the device wouldn't slide down the track when the engine wheels hit it. I decided it was time for me to explode my first cap, so I placed it on the railroad track and dropped a large rock on it. The cap exploded, sending sand from the bottom of the cap onto my chest, arms, and face. I wasn't hurt too bad, but after this dumb move, we left the other caps where we found them and decided it was time to go home.

During the four years I went to Woodstock School, I never entered the lunchroom. Lunch was 15 cents per day and a carton of milk was 5 cents for those who brought their lunch from home in brown bags. In the early 1940s, there weren't any metal lunch boxes yet. I spent every lunch hour on the outside play equipment, never being questioned by school staff. Dad left 75 cents on the kitchen table every Monday for me to buy 5 meals. Having nothing and having money, I spent it all every Monday in the stores along Woodstock Boulevard on the mile-long walk I had to school. I bought candy bars at 5 cents each, metal toy cars and trucks at 10 cents each and fireworks during the month prior to the 4th of July. Cherry bombs (a device the size of a plum) were 5 cents and could be thrown to the sidewalk where they would explode. Ladyfingers (very small firecrackers that you could hold in your-hand while they were exploding) were 10 cents per strand.

We took our fireworks to our foxhole to set them off as we weren't sup-posed to have them. For 5 cents, I'd buy a red firecracker three inches long with a half inch diameter and a red fuse. We had a tin can stored at our fox hole and would light the 'Big Blockbuster' under the can and blow it up about twenty feet in the air. When we ran out of fireworks, we raided Dad's cupboard at home and took several .22 caliber shells. With a pair of plyers, I pulled the lead bullet out of the shell and dumped the black powder on a 2-foot-long 2"x6" wooden board. We then set the black powder on fire and struck it with a hammer, exploding it with a loud bang.

Using my dime toy cars and trucks that I purchased with my school lunch money, I would build a city with streets, bridges, and parking lots using the dirt under a big lilac bush beside our house. I spent hours doing this. Lilac was my mom's favorite flower, and it turned out to be mine as well. I left my cars outside so I did not have to explain where they came from. I lost all my cars and trucks the last year we lived in Portland over a dumb idea I had. I held a carnival in our backyard and invited all the local kids to attend. Seven or eight kids attended. I made tossing games out of cardboard boxes, rocks, and lines in the dirt. I sold rides on a borrowed bike for 5 cents each. Another game I set up was a ring toss game. In school, under the supervision of my teacher, I spent several days making a toy. We worked on our handcrafted project for about one hour per day. The teacher gave us a piece of plywood that was ¼ inch thick, 10 inches by 10 inches, and a pattern of a clown's face with a funny long nose. We used a coping saw to cut the face out and then painted it. The object of the game was to hold the clown's head by the skinny neck and toss a plywood ring about 3 inches around, attached to the end of the clown's nose by a string to get the ring to fall over the nose. It was hard to master a 'ringer'. My carnival customers liked this game the best. It upset me when I found out my dad had left this toy behind when we moved to Tillamook County. Another game I had was a rock toss into a 10-inch circle I made in the dirt. The player had to remain behind a line 10 feet away when tossing a rock. There weren't many winners here. The game looked easier than it was. All my friends had fun for about three hours. My dad was sleep-ing because he worked nights, and Mom just thought I had a lot of friends over. I used my toy cars for prizes. After the carnival, I ended up with less than $2 and no toys left.

Another moneymaker gone bad started off with two hazelnut trees growing wild beside our street, across from our house and 300 feet to the North. I planned on picking nuts and selling them door to door like I had done with cherries and produce. I crawled under the low hanging tree limbs and found most of the nuts were on the ground. Most of the nuts had tiny wormholes in them, and the shells were empty. After crawling back out of the brush, I began to itch on my hands, arms, and face. The short brush under the nut trees was Poison Oak.

While in the 3rd grade at Woodstock school, my best friend was a classmate named Norman. One day Norman and I were the first ones back to the classroom following A.M. recess. As we walked to our desks, which were in the back of the room, I saw Norman pick up a dime that was lying on a desk, and put it in his shirt pocket. After the entire class returned to their desks, a girl started crying and when asked by the teacher why, she said somebody took her dime that was her lunch milk money. School lunches cost 15 cents and milk in a pint carton was 5 cents. Students bought milk to go with their sack lunches brought from home in the event they did not want the school hot lunch. The teacher asked who had returned to the room from recess first, and Norman and I had to raise our hands.

The teacher came to the back of the classroom and told Norman and me to empty our pockets and turn them inside out. I turned my empty pockets out. While the teacher was watching me, that gave Norman time to put the dime in his left shoe. When the teacher did not find the dime, she told us to take our shoes off. The teacher watched as I removed my shoes, then there was a knock on the classroom door that the teacher had to go answer. At the door was the mother of a sick classmate who came to pick up homework for her son. With the teacher's back turned towards us, Norman took the dime from his shoe and swallowed it. Not finding the dime, the teacher started with our studies again. At lunchtime, I found Norman on the swing set. He told me he had not gone to the lunchroom because he was going to die from eating the dime.

In the 3rd grade, with WWII raging on, I liked to spend my spare time in the classroom drawing military airplanes. My favorite was an Army Air Corps P-38 Fighter with its nose and wing guns blazing (there was no U.S. Airforce yet). My teacher knew about my drawing and also knew my friend Norman was a better artist than me. When Christmas was only a week away, she asked me and Norman if we would draw Christmas decorations on all the chalkboards in the room using colored chalk. We drew for about 4 hours while our class did their usual studies. I worked slowly to allow Norman to do three-fourths of the work, knowing he was a much better artist. I drew snowmen, Christmas trees, bells, and wreaths. Our drawings turned out good and our teacher thanked us.

On my first day of school in the fourth grade, my teacher told the class that they would choose three boys to become safety patrol officers and for those interested to raise their hands. My hand went up. After the class was told that the boys selected would need to come to school half an hour early and stay half an hour late every day, most of the hands went down. They appointed me and two other boys to the school crosswalk safety program, issuing us a green armband that read, 'Safety Patrol,' a white canvas three inch wide belt that went over our left shoulder then around our waist and a nice silver colored badge that read, 'Portland Junior Safety Patrol.' At 3:30 that afternoon, I reported to my assigned crosswalk for what became a week of training by 5th and 6th grade boys who had been in the school crosswalk program for a year or more. Before going on duty, we picked up a handheld sign that read, 'Stop' on one side and 'Slow' on the other side. I enjoyed my new position and little did I know I would wear a badge for 20 years as a law enforcement officer later in life. My younger brother wasn't very excited about my new position because he had to come to school a half hour early and stay a half hour late with me as he was too young to walk to and from school by himself (he was in 2nd grade).

On the last day of school, the teacher handed out our report cards. I had passed onto the 5th grade. They called me to the front of the class and presented me with my badge and green armband with white lettering reading, 'Safety Patrol' as keepsakes for doing a good job and not missing one day of crossing guard for the entire year. I still own the badge and armband. My Mom was very impressed and after sheriff's cars stopped our family's car at a roadblock, on our move to Tillamook County, she said, "You should have showed them your badge." I was very proud.

We rarely had family outings as a rule. When I was 10 and my brother was 8 we were allowed to go with my dad and his friend, who was in his mid-30s to watch them fish in the Willamette River. On one of these trips to watch them fish, my brother fell off the high bank into the river. The current carried him about 30 feet out and slowly downstream. He floated with his head bobbing underwater and then on top again. Dad's friend ran down the river

Gordon Lee's Portland Junior Safety Patrol badge.

Gordon Lee's Portland Junior Safety Patrol arm band.

after my brother, yelling and pointing, then dove into the water ahead of my brother. He swam out and met him floating downstream. The man grabbed ahold of my brother's shirt collar and swam, pulling him to shore, saving his life. After the rescued, we headed home without fishing that day.

My brother had another close call when he found a gallon jug filled with kerosene under the kitchen sink and drank about a glass full. They rushed him to the hospital, where his stomach was pumped. The hospital staff held him overnight for observation. My brother had another stay at the hospital after that for an emergency operation to have his appendix removed. When that happened, they sent me to our neighbors', Mr. and Mrs. Dickson, to spend a couple of nights. I slept between sheets instead of my surplus army blankets for the first time in my life. The sheets felt very good, but strange. While at the hospital, the staff gave my brother a piggy bank. The doctor, nurses and any visitors put coins in the piggy which sat on his bedside stand. When he returned home, he and I would play on the living room floor with all of his coins. We would have fun stacking and counting them. We had never seen so much money before. Thinking back, he probably had between 10 and 15 dollars. I do not recall what he did with his money.

Somehow, Mom found out Dad was having an affair with a female welder he worked with at the shipyard. Her name was Edna. After confronting Dad, Mom found glass chips on her food, so she called the police from a neighbor's phone as we didn't own one then. Two Portland policemen arrived and said they were going to interview us all. I was only about 9 years old and scared, so I ran out the back door and climbed up the Bing cherry tree. The police stood under the tree and spent about a half hour trying to talk me down, to no avail, so they finally gave up and left the area.

When I came down Mom told me the police found out Dad had cut glass while on his job and chips fell onto his clothing, then from his clothing onto the food. Mom lost the entire side of her family over a previous experience with glass in food that was very traumatic. I was living on my grandparents' farm in Creighton, Nebraska, when it happened, so they did not invite me to the Thanksgiving dinner that Mom, Dad, and my year-old brother attended at the Pratt house. Mom's relationship with her dad, Charles Pratt, was not the best to begin with, because before Mom got married, she lived at home and Charles took her paychecks from the Omaha Hospital for room and board. When Mom married, Mr. Pratt lost his cash cow and was angry. The Pratts said they found chips of glass in their Thanksgiving dinner and that my mom and dad had done it. They kicked my Mom, Dad, and my broth-er out of the house and banned them from ever contacting the Pratts in any manner again. My Mom never talked to, wrote to or saw any of her family again. She had a brother named Clayton, a younger brother named Donald, and a sister named Bonnie who used to babysit me when I was a year old. I never knew my grandmother's first name, as I left Omaha when I was only 22 months old. (Her name was Anna Stolgran Pratt, found in 2019 in online re-cords). This family breakup entered into the plans for Mom and Dad to take us kids to Oregon to live. Others considered Charles Pratt a 'low life' type. One time, Mom's brother Donald was in trouble with the law and had stolen a .45 automatic handgun from the front seat of a parked police car that he gave to my dad because he was afraid to get caught with it. Dad kept it in his bedroom cupboard for lots of years. I do not know where the stolen gun is now. Perhaps my brothers know where it is. Bonnie came to visit Mom when she was on her deathbed in a Tillamook rest home. Mom said her sister stayed for about an hour. The answer to any question I had about my mom's family was, "I don't want to talk about it." I do not know what Grandpa Charles Pratt did for a liv-ing. All the Pratt relations Mom knew would be dead by now.

When Mom found out Dad was having an affair with Edna, she was told he wanted to remain with his family. Then Mom insisted that the family have a professional photo taken. I have a copy of the photo that shows me at age 10 with a big patch of eczema on my cheek. They gave me cow's milk as a newborn baby which caused eczema so badly it hospitalized me. Mom said my sores wept so much that I would stick to the bedding. Late one night, they called Mom and Dad to the hospital and told them I wouldn't live until morning. Mom prayed to God and said that if He spared me, I would become a minister of God. To help keep Mom's word, I became ordained as a minister of the Universal Life Church on October 8, 2003. I am authorized to perform the rites of the church, including wed-dings, funerals, baptisms, and blessings. In the state of Oregon, I have all the rights given to members of the clergy. My only religious function I have performed to date was to baptize my friend Rene's ashes that I took and spread in Yellowstone Park at her request.

One night, Dad left for work and then returned home by 1 a.m., an hour and a half after leaving for work. Dad woke Mom up and told her the war had ended, the shipyard was closed, and he no longer had a job. Since he was used to being at work all night and sleeping days, he could not go to

The family photo that was taken in 1942-43. Gordon Lee is 10 in this photo.

bed and was leaving with a fellow employee of the shipyard and going to Manzanita in Tillamook County on a fishing trip, to look for a new job and a place for us all to live. When he returned home, he said he had found a job at Buel Hardware in Tillamook at $1.52 per hour and had rented a two-bedroom cabin for us to live in beside the Barview store in Barview, Oregon. We were on our way to cheese, trees, and ocean breeze.

Dad also told Mom that his friend Edna wanted him to go to Texas with her, but he said no, so she had left Oregon to return to her home state of Texas. He kept a plastic framed photo of her in his toolbox from that day on. Mom and I both saw the picture in the 1950s, but she never brought that fact up to Dad. I hoped living on the Oregon coast would be a better life for us.

The Tillamook Burn.

Tillamook County, Oregon
1945

We moved to Tillamook County in July of 1945. I was allowed to do anything within reason and come and go, day or night, without any questions. I tried not to violate my parents' trust or get in trouble with the law and did nothing wrong other than the usual kid stuff. After we moved, I never saw my dad take a drink again except for a beer or two on TV wrestling night.

We took Highway 6, the Wilson River Highway, through the Tillamook Burn when moving to Barview, to our temporary house. The Tillamook Burn had burned every six years for a couple of decades for some reason or other. 1939 was the last big fire, so it was due the year we moved in 1945. We didn't get over 15 miles into Tillamook County before we were driving through smoke. The mountainside on the north side of Highway 6 was burning big time. We came upon a sheriff's car roadblock. There was a forestry bus beside the road and three or four sheriff cars. The sheriff checked Dad's license and told him we could continue with caution. The deputy also said all males over 18 with no children in their vehicle or a female who couldn't drive had to get on the bus and fight fire or get into the backseat of a patrol car and go to jail as an emergency had been declared. A logging outfit had started the fire by accident when two cables used for pulling logs up a mountain using a spar tree had rubbed together, causing enough heat to start the fire. The loggers involved helped fight the fire, which burned for several square miles. This was the third time the Tillamook Burn had burned. There was also a fourth fire in 1951. Over 72 million seedlings were planted in this area in a major reforestation effort between 1949 and 1972. One million of these were hand planted by young people from Northwest Oregon. The Tillamook Burn was later dedicated as the Tillamook State Forest by Governor Tom McCall in 1973.

We arrived in Barview, Oregon, where Dad had rented us a two-bedroom cabin right beside the Barview Store (after becoming a builder years later, Dad remodeled this store. It was a magnificent building after his remodel).

There were three or four cabins facing north, just two blocks from the ocean and one block from a large sand hill, which was about a city block tall. The hill is still there, but it has eroded to be about 80% of what it used to be from people playing on it. The county has now turned the area into a county park with overnight camping for a fee and day use, which is free. My brother and I played on the hill every day for the two months that we lived in Barview. We stayed away from the dangerous ocean. I do not recall ever going into the store as us kids had zero money. Mom stayed in the cabin the entire time, as she was PG. We could not say the word 'pregnant' as that word was considered too sexual in those days. Mom gave birth to my youngest brother in September, less than 90 days after our move to Tillamook County.

During the daytime, Dad planned on working as a store clerk at minimum wage, and in his spare time he read and studied from small how-to black books to learn how to build homes, starting with our house in Bay City. He read every night and purchased tools at Buel Hardware so he could become a builder. Dad worked his job as a hardware store clerk and spent his nights and weekends building a one-room house on the Bay City property before school started the first week of September, with Mom giving birth the third week. The property was 6 acres on Warren Street, just across the railroad tracks and about four blocks east of Tillamook Bay. In later times, if kids wanted to be mean, they said, "Oh, you live on the mudflats," which I felt was an insult. Dad purchased the property at Walt Pettey's real estate office in Bay City. In years past, the property had been the city park. The land was logged back about 200 feet from the gravel road and logs were pushed into a pile that was about 30 feet tall and a city block long. Five acres or so were covered in salmonberry and both blue and red huckleberries. We all loved the property over the years but found out after the purchase that no plants or brush could be cut or removed because someone observed a spotted owl on the property. Nothing could be done with the other 5 acres but pay the taxes on it because the land was protected. There weren't any water or electrical services on the street then.

In five weeks Dad completed the one-room house, which was later the living room, and we moved in just prior to the school year opening. He dug an outhouse hole and built an outhouse which we had to use for 3 or 4 years because there weren't any water pipes installed on Warren Street yet. Our address was 'Rt 1 Box 126' and changed in later years to 7900 Warren Street. My best friend Jerry H. (mentioned later in this book) went from RFD to 7900 Baseline.

Over the next few months, Dad added to the house, building three bedrooms, a family room, a kitchen, and a game room, as well as a long-awaited bathroom. In the meantime, we all ate, slept, and lived in one room. I slept on my army cot made of canvas with board slats on each side that hurt my arms during the night if I was not careful. In the evenings, Mom would play old-time games with us like describing a thing in the room, and we had to guess what it was. One time, Mom's question that stumped us was, "What is black and white and red all over?" The answer was a newspaper. We also had a large 2' x 2' Philco radio to listen to.

Dad added a large room on the Northeast corner of the house that got converted 2 years later into a kitchen, but sat empty with no use until 1949 or so. Billy and I would lie in the empty room on the floor and listen to our special programs on the radio seven nights per week from after dinner until it was time for bed. There was no TV yet, but we enjoyed the programs, with their sound effects, just as much as a TV show. We had about 30 or more shows we loved to hear such as:

Red Rider

Amos 'n' Andy

Lone Ranger

The Shadow

The Baby Snooks Show

The Roy Rogers Show

Lum and Abner

Hopalong Cassidy

We also listened to all the Portland Beaver baseball games, both at home and away. Years later I was very disappointed to learn Bob Blackburn and

Rollie Truitt never left Portland for the away games. They read a teletype to find out what was taking place and then re-created the game using crowd taped noise and would hit a pencil on a desk for hits and foul ball sound effects. Later, when I was 13 and Billy was 11, we hitchhiked to Portland to attend the Beaver's ball games, which ended at about 11 p.m. Then we hitch-hiked home and got there about 1 a.m. Mom and Dad let us do what we wanted, so long as we never got in trouble. One night going home, two drunk men picked us up and drove so badly I was afraid. I told them to let us out in the middle of nowhere in the Tillamook Burn, 30 miles from home, which they did.

We earned our own money for treats and ballgame entry fees in vari-ous ways. We never earned an allowance. Dad gave Mom an allowance of $20 per month and expected her to buy everything she needed on that small amount. The entire 9 years I lived with her and Dad in Bay City, Mom never owned any:

stockings, underpants, coats, slippers, hats, rainwear, jewelry, watches, bed clothing, or a robe. She only had one pair of $2.99 flats (shoes), only two cotton floral print house dresses, one bra, and limited cosmetics.

While growing up from age 2 to age 11, I had no: allowance, undershorts or undershirts, coat, hat or other rainwear, toothbrush or toothpaste, sweats, sweat socks or knee pads for sports, no jockstrap, washrags to wash my face (we were expected to use the corner of a towel), or good hair oil. Growing up, I wanted a bottle of Wild Root so bad but only had a 10-cent jar of Fitch hair oil that was just like Wesson oil and ran down my face. I didn't own a nail clipper, so I developed hangnails. My friend Bill Lane's mom noticed my nails, gave me some clippers, clipped my hangnails and showed me how to take care of them.

In 1961 and 1963, at age 25 and 27, I had to have all my upper and lower teeth pulled. I then began wearing upper and lower dentures. Due to lack of good quality food I was significantly underweight growing up. I only had breakfast cereal for breakfast and we never had lunch except for school lunch. 90 percent of the time the cold cereal was corn flakes. I don't remem-ber ever having juice, ham, bacon, eggs, toast, hash browns, cocoa, etc. un-til I left home. My salvation was the hot lunches served at school at 15 cents per lunch, which Dad provided. Unlike Woodstock school, I never missed a

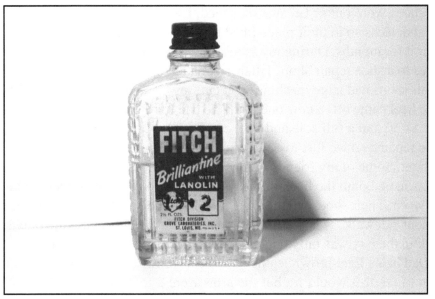

A bottle of Fitch Hair Oil.

what about buying toy cars etc., instead?

hot lunch if I was in school. On the weekends where I had no school lunch, I never had more than white bread with salad dressing only on it. In late August, Dad took us to Tillamook to JC Penney Company and bought us 2 shirts, 2 pairs of jeans, 2 socks, and the cheapest pair of shoes that fit. One time my shoes were cheap red tractor tread shoes that I was ashamed to wear. He didn't buy me any underwear, a coat or a hat. In the summer, when the shoes wore out or became damaged, I went barefoot. One time I broke my shoelaces so in their place I had to use fishing line from the garage and wear it for months. During my school days, most people took their worn-out shoes to a shoe repair shop. Tillamook had a repair shop on 2nd Street. The repair shops had large machines that cut, sewed, and buffed leather. When a shoe heel came off, a new one could be had for $.35 to $.50 cents. A ½ sole was $1.50 and a full sole and heel cost $3.00. My dad would never pay for shoe repairs, so we just tossed our damaged shoes in the garbage and went without. Some of my friends in school paid $.25 cents per shoe to have steel cleats nailed onto the back of their shoe heels so the rubber heel would not get worn. Their shoes would make a clicking noise when they walked on a cement sidewalk. This wasn't a big deal in Bay City because the only side-walk in the city was only one block long in front of Decker's store.

Dad had a light brown leather coat he never wore in his closet and I tried it on to see if it would fit, but the arms were 2 to 3 inches too long. When my dad finished building my bedroom, I had to share it with Billy. Both of us had a used iron Goodwill bed with two wool army blankets and one homemade dresser made with ¼ inch unpainted plywood with drilled holes in the drawers that were used to open it. When you placed your fingers in the holes, the rough drilled wood gave you slivers in your fingers. We didn't need a closet because we didn't own coats and only had 2 pairs of jeans and 2 shirts each, which meant we had one on and one in the wash. Mom had a Maytag washing machine with a wringer. She would wash our clothes and then hang them on a clothesline. Sometimes clothing did not get dry outside overnight, so we wore damp clothing to school. Occasionally I put my pants over the oil heater stove in the living room before leaving for school, but that made them stiff and hard to wear.

One time, a local businessman, who knew our family well, thought it was hilarious that he saw Billy and me walking Highway 101 with our gunny sacks between Bay City and Garibaldi picking up soda and beer bottles for the refund. Billy and I could walk the Highway from Bay City to Hobson-

Map of Bay City Oregon

Map of Bay City, Oregon along Tillamook Bay.
Image courtesy of Google / Google Maps and Data Partners: NAVTEQ
& TeleAtlas (2020).

ville in 4 or 5 hours and get $4 or so at Normo's store for the bottles we found.

The refund rates were:

1 cent for beer stubbies

2 cents for small sodas

3 cents for Dad's Root Beer quarts

5 cents for all other quart-sized soda bottles

Bay City, Oregon
1945

The business district was roughly 4 to 5 times larger, from 1910 to 1939, than it is today. I have photos of all the standing commercial buildings in 1918.

A Bay City Poster Read:

> 'Come to Bay City, Oregon
> Greatest Future of Any Town in Oregon
> Mills
> Railroads
> Factories'

Bay City's Charter was established in 1910. Today Bay City is known as the Pearl of Tillamook Bay because of all of its Oyster beds. It sits on the east side of Tillamook Bay. The elevation of the small city that thrived as a mill and fishing town is 17 feet above sea level. Shortly after the turn of the 19th century, the city had declined to a sleepy village with seafood being its leading industry. In 2010, Bay City's population was 1286 according to the census. Scott Cone platted the town in late 1888 after his hometown in Michigan. Cone and C.E. Wilson were partners in the timber business and bought the property Bay City sat on for $100 dollars. They purchased 52 acres of land from George W. and Martha Jacoby, which the Jacobys had purchased from Martha's uncle, John Monroe. He, in turn, had inherited it from an earlier settler, Obet S. Thomas, in 1882.

The city limit signs on both ends of town in 1945 listed the population as 390. In the early days, when the population changed, boards were placed over the numbers and the new numbers were listed. When I went into the U.S. Marine Corps in 1953 the population sign of Bay City still read 390, but there were at least 761 people living there then.

Bay City view from the bay.

Bay City Methodist Church where I attended.

When we moved to Bay City in 1945 there were the following commercial buildings:

Going north, the first business on the east side of Highway 101, one block or less off of the bay and 2 blocks south of City Center, was a Texaco Station with living quarters, which also sold penny candy and cheap toys.

Two blocks north on Highway 101 on the west side of the highway overlooking the bay was a Chevon Service Station, ran by a man named Harvey.

200 feet north on the same side of the highway, there was a tiny post office connected to Jack Decker's grocery. The post office was perhaps 30 feet wide and 60 feet long. It was open for business from 8 a.m. to 5 p.m., but the lobby remained open 24/7 for access to ink pens and post boxes.

Decker's store was quite large, with living quarters attached to the north side. The store also had two other apartments attached to it. At the end of the block, but facing D Street, was the Methodist church. The next block going north had houses on both sides of the highway. Then came a bigger grocery store called Bay City Grocery and Market ran by Howard Normo, who was a very nice person with many very good business ideas, including a free weekly drawing for about 50 things. He urged customers to sign their store receipts and place them in a large box for the drawing each Friday night. About 60 people would attend these drawings. I would suspect the prizes were his slow-moving stock items. Mr. Normo also purchased our hand-picked wild blackberries. We picked evergreen blackberries, which were small, and on green and red shrubs and Himalayan blackberries which were 2 times as big as the evergreen blackberries. The usual price paid to us was 5 cents per pound. We earned about $2 to $3 for a good day's work. A truck picked up the berries from Mr. Normo each evening. We also sold foxglove (Digitalis, which is used for heart medication) at 5 to 7 cents per pound. We used knives to cut the plants and gunny sacks to carry the plants. Foxglove grew all over in the foothills above Bay City on logging cat roads. We also peeled cascara bark for 7 cents per pound and 21 cents if we dried it out, but if dried it lost about half its weight. Mr. Normo kept all of his fruit and vegetables on tables outside, along the entire front area of his store unsupervised day and night. Hardly anything was ever damaged or stolen.

Across the highway from Normo's store was Ben Scheelar's Hardware (all new) and Appliance (some new and some used). Ben was a good friend to me and my dad. Ben lived in an apartment above his store. Dad would stop at Ben's store to buy nails and other things, saving him a trip to Tillamook. Every day at high tide, during daylight hours, Ben put a sign on the front door that read, 'Gone Fishing.' Ben, with a fishing pole in hand, walked his dog the 3 blocks to the Bay City docks and fished. Ben told me of an abandoned oyster bed in the Bay at the end of the street I lived on. Sure enough, I had free oysters from then on. Ben also kept an eye on Mr. Normo's produce outside the grocery store for him from his apartment window that overlooked Highway 101.

In the next block, north of Normo's store on the same side of the street was a drive-thru clam chowder booth which was only open during tourist season, 11 a.m. to dark. Drive-thru chowder was $1 per large paper cup with a plastic spoon. That was the only product they sold. Brownies' Tavern walocated behind the chowder stand on Fourth Street at B Street. I never went inside Brownies' Tavern while growing up.

About half-a-mile south of the city center on the bay was Bay City Boat Works, where boats were built in a large building, about one and a half times as big as a large dairy barn. Some new boats they built were very large and used in the ocean. There was a 150-foot-long wooden launch that extended out of the boat building and into the bay. The wood launch was greased and newly built boats were pushed out of the building and into the bay at high tide. My Dad helped them build a very large ocean-going boat in 1951 and received a free ride to Astoria, Oregon on the new boat. Dad returned to Bay City on the Oregon Bus Line. For his part-time work, he received a 3-inch-thick, 6-inch-square mahogany board. He constructed it into a round living room table 18 inches tall and 5 feet across. We used the table for playing cards in the living room.

The Oregon Stage Line was in business prior to Greyhound Bus Company. The stage line had no depot in Tillamook County, nor did it have any regular bus stops. The stage traveled Hwy 101 and stopped for passengers whenever they were standing beside the highway where there was enough safe space to pullover. The riders would flag the stage down by waving their arm. After telling the driver your destination, you were told what the fee was. All rides were cash only, paid to the driver. I never rode on the stage line, electing to travel for free by hitchhiking.

On the south-side of the boat works was an abandoned barn. Some hay bales were stored on a side lean-to building. A family from Texas moved into the barn and had an open cooking fire and sleeping bags on a dirt floor on the north end. I visited the Smith family often, ate meals with them and played in the hay with their 4 or 5 kids, two of which were around my age. The Smith family lived in the barn for the better part of a year before moving on. On the west side of Fourth Street, which is now a city park, sat a large Odd Fellows Hall, with a very large floor area at street level. Live music, dances, cakewalks, and picnic basket auctions, among other functions, were held in this building. The midnight football games were my favorite. The appointed team captains chose the two teams. One team placed their back to the west wall and the other team had their backs to the east wall. They turned the lights out so it was pitch black in the building. One of the two referees with flashlights placed a ball in the center of the room, turned off the flashlight and said, "Go." The first team member to locate the ball and take it to the other team's wall yelled, "GOAL!" and the game was over. There were no other rules, so it got rough. They also played poker card games in the building.

Prior to WWII, when it was discontinued, the tourist event Bay City was known for was an annual oyster festival held across from the city docks on the east side of the street. A trench about 3 feet wide, 2 feet deep and 50 feet long was dug and a wood fire was started to produce hot coals for cooking the oysters. After the flames went out and while the coals were red hot, saltwater-soaked gunny sacks of fresh oysters were lowered into the trench and covered with soil to cook. The oysters, still in their shells, were uncovered and sold to the tourists and Bay City residents. Many cars would stop and park near the oyster trench to see what was going on.

Hayes Oyster Company had oyster beds on Tillamook Bay, and sold fresh and canned oysters. The Hayes family lived on Highway 101 a few feet south of Normo's store and were also family friends.

Bay City had a very good volunteer fire department. To report a fire, you would call phone number 346. To bring the volunteer firefighters to the fire department, they sounded a very loud siren that could be heard over the entire city, and perhaps a mile beyond. They activated the siren about one or two times per month on average. Many residents of Bay City would wonder where the fire was located and made a point to check the Bay City News section of the Headlight Herald for fire information. The closest ambulance service was in Tillamook, six miles south of Bay City, using Hwy 101. The new section of Hwy 101 was not in place yet, which made the distance only five miles now. The two ambulance services were Lundberg & Son Mortuary, Phone #30 and Waud's Funeral Home, Phone #31. Both ambulance companies were in the city of Tillamook.

Candlestick and Baldy Mountain, in plain view from most of Bay City, were logged off in the 1930s-40s. Mt. Baldy was completely bare and Candlestick was bare except for one spar tree standing alone at the very top. Spar trees had cables attached near the top. A gas driven 'donkey' pulls the logs up the hill after loggers called 'choker setters' attached cables to the logs to be pulled. An air horn attached to the choker setters' belt was sounded after a cable, also called cable wire rope, used to pull the logs was in place and everyone in the area was in the clear, to avoid injuries. The donkey operator then sounded his air horn and started the pull.

Baldy and Candlestick could clearly be seen from Bay City for several years until brush grew up and hid most of the view. Spar trees were typically removed after an area was logged and either used again at the next work site or loaded on a log truck and taken to a sawmill to be sawed into lumber. Candlestick's spar tree was the only spar tree left standing on a work site I ever saw in Tillamook County.

The predecessor to the Port of Tillamook Bay Railroad was a line built by Pacific Railway and Navigation Company between 1906 and 1911. PR&N Railroad had 91 miles of track and made 34 stops between Hillsboro and Tillamook, which cost $5.57 per adult. A one-way trip took 5 hours and 35 minutes. PR&N was later sold to Southern Pacific Railroad. Southern Pacific Railroad owned the railroad track from Portland to Hillsboro and a Southern Pacific engine was used to pull the PR&N cars from Portland to Hillsboro. A PR&N steam train engine pulled the cars on the PR&N track from Hillsboro to Tillamook. Some folks called the PR&N "Punk, Rotten, and Nasty" because of the wet and muddy working conditions of crews building the railroad through the Coast Range and that smoke and soot entered the passenger cars from the steam engine causing problems (dirty clothing and bodies). As of November 10, 1911, there were 3 trains per day from Portland to Tillamook. According to a flyer for Train #142 in 1911, that train's schedule was:

Leave Portland	7:20 a.m.
Hillsboro	8:50 a.m.
Bay City	Arrive 1:45 p.m.
Tillamook	Arrive 2:25 p.m.

Bay City Train Depot.

Bay City School.

Part II
Bay City Grade School
1946 ~ 1950

5th Grade
1946 ~ 1947

On Opening Day of our new school where I started the 5th grade and Billy the 3rd, we walked the three quarters of a mile or so an hour early as we were excited. Bill's teacher was Mrs. Hoskins, and mine was Goldie Fogg. There were two grades to a classroom that shared a teacher. 1st and 2nd, 3rd and 4th, 5th and 6th, and 7th and 8th. The high school took up the balance of the space.

Every morning we started off with the Pledge of Allegiance. Our teacher would teach two classes at one time, putting one side of the classroom to work and then starting on the other side. We all had old-time desks with full ink wells and a slot on the top of the desk to hold the ink pen, which used a replaceable nib for writing. The school district furnished all books. As I was the new student in class, the teacher asked me to stand and tell the class a little about myself. For some reason, the teacher became delighted when I told the class I had lived in Milwaukie, Oregon and the reason they named it that was because there was a mill that had a walkway around it and on the walk was a key. I thought it was kind of corny, so followed up with the fact that just up the street from our home was the Bomber Gas Station. There was a WW2 Boeing B-17G Bomber Airplane on the station's canopy covering the gas pumps. The B-17G garnered lots of attention from the public and was used for years as an advertisement. This story of mine caught the attention of all the boys present. The real war bomber remained at the gas station for several years but it has since been removed. Over the years, the old aircraft became more valuable than the gas station and efforts to restore it to its original flying glory have come underway.

Mr. Art Lacey owned the large commercial property which included a Texaco gas station consisting of four islands of gas pumps with 18 employees all wearing white uniform coveralls, as well as a motel and the Bomber Restaurant. A sign on the property read,

The Bomber Gas Station.

'Entering Bomber City

Population 50,000 or Less'

        In 1947, Mr. Art Lacey purchased the B-17G long-range bomber for
$5,000 at an Oklahoma airbase. Art won a $5 bet from a friend who said he
couldn't do it. There are only about 40 B-17 flying fortress/sky chiefs left and
only a few that are airworthy. The B-17 remained as the gas station canopy
for just short of 70 years when it was taken to a Salem, Oregon airport hangar,
to be restored and then placed in Art Lacey's grandsons' WW2 museum along
with many other WW2 collectibles, most of which were donated by veterans.
Art called his B-17 'Lacey Lady'. The museum is called, The B-17 Alliance
Museum & Restoration Hanger.
        The Bay City school was a two-story building on the side of a small hill
with the second story at street level on the west end and the first story at
street level on the east end because of the way the hill was shaped prior to the
building being there. The main front door was on the west end so you could
enter the school on the upper floor with the office on the front left. The High
School Study Hall and three classrooms were on the upper floor. Study Hall
was a large room that held all students in 9th through 12th grade. A County
LPN (nurse) visited two to three days per school year and gave all students
in the grade school and high school a quick physical checkup lasting about
10 minutes. The 5th and 6th combined classroom was at the right southwest
corner. 7th and 8th grade were at the northwest corner of the second floor. The
3rd and 4th grade combined room was at the far east of the 2nd floor, past
the High School rooms. The 1st and 2nd grade room was on the first floor on
the east end of the building. There were three kids in 12th grade, ten kids in
11th grade, seven kids in 10th grade, and eleven kids in 9th grade. There were
four high school teachers and four grade school teachers. A ramped walkway
covered with a rubber rug for safety led from the 2nd floor near the west end
front of the building down to the first floor, which contained the dining room
ran by Mrs. Ramsey who cooked all the food. She was a wonderful cook and
also made bread and desserts. An indoor gym and play area took up most of
the remaining room on the 1st floor. The gym only had one basketball hoop
and which was used when it was too wet to go outside. The gym also had a
built-in full-size stage that would serve a variety of other uses, such as grad-

uation. They would set the stage up with chairs facing it. Back in those days, boys and girls received a diploma for grade school graduation. On the far east end of the gym, a 30-foot stairway led down to a basement containing a boiler and asbestos covered pipes that went to all the schoolroom radiators. The pipes were about 3 inches around with 10 to 12 inches of Asbestos wrapped around them. Mr. Ramsey, the cook's husband, and school janitor, also had his tools, supplies, and an office there. The teachers also had a smoking area down there, as they were not allowed to smoke in front of any students. About 50 feet east of the schoolhouse was a larger 3-story gym. At that time, it was the best gym in the county. There was a 3-inch-thick climbing rope suspended from the ceiling (about 40 feet long with no safety mat). The ground level floor had bleacher seating overlooking a hardwood basketball court. The bleachers could seat about 300 people. The gym had a porch and ticket sales windows on both ends of the building facing north toward the city street. Down a stairway on the northwest end, there was a large girls' locker and shower room. On the southwest side, down a stairway, was the boys' locker and shower room. This is where I had my first shower. I never had a shower at home.

Behind the school and the gym was a play area with swings. We played marbles (for keeps) and King of the Mountain just behind the school building, which was about a city block long. Playing King of the Mountain on the side hill entailed having a big partner to carry you on his shoulders and run while other players tried to knock them to the ground (anything goes). My partner was the biggest kid in the class, Ken Crawford, known by his nickname 'Tank'. We usually won.

In 1945, when I started the 5th grade at Bay City Grade School, I overheard some boys talking about a comic book store in a lady's house. The house was in a line of older small homes just south of Hayes Oyster Street and faced Tillamook Bay, about a city block east from where Hwy 101 sits now. They moved the highway from the city's main business district two blocks east.

Comic Books were very much in demand by children, as there wasn't television in Tillamook County at the time. The lady's home sat alongside a few other homes which are now all gone, and they turned the area into a marshland. I went to the Comic lady's home and found she had turned her living room into a used comic store. New books in the local stores sold for 10 cents at the time. The lady's used books sold for 5 cents each, but she would rather trade you one of her books for two of your books. The room had hundreds of comics, which were all sorted and displayed by the comic's names. Her inventory increased every day. It was fun to just visit her store and view the books. For reasons unknown to me, the comic book store closed, and the lady moved after a few short months.

'The goat lady', aka 'Walking Annie', would walk by our house a couple of times per day. The old dirty looking lady had built a one-room shack out of driftwood on the bay and lived with several goats. Nobody wanted anything to do with her. Mom would motion for her to come to our patio table and eat a meal she had saved for her. Then Mom would go inside while Annie walked to the table because she was worried about what others would think if they saw her with the 'the goat lady'. This was a frequent occurrence.

Just across the highway from our house was another house where a lady would watch from her window whenever Billy and I were in the front yard. One time we decided to put on a show for her and staged a fight with knockdowns, play choking, and other things. We thought she would call the police, but she didn't. She got even with me without even knowing anything about it. One day, a block above her house on the top of a hill where no one could see me, I decided to take a leak. The lady had a two-wire electric fence. The idea was to pee on the fence, which turned out to be a big mistake. The shock from the fence knocked me down. The lady's cow was amused.

The railroad tracks were a big part of my life growing up. Log trains pulled by steam engines went by daily. Some trains were over a mile long, with two engines pulling and one pushing. Each flatcar carried two logs on the bottom and another resting between the bottom two. An exception to this was when a flatcar had only one 8 to 10-foot diameter old growth log on it. Two-man handcars that carried railroad workers by pumping a lever, and larger ones that we called 'speeders' with a gas engine that carried 6 to 8 railroad men went by daily. These men worked on the railroad right of way. All the railroad trestles and bridges had 55-gallon drums with a bucket on a hook to put out fires caused by sparks from the firebox of the steam trains. They filled the drums to the top with water and checked them regularly. I would often walk on a rail from my house to downtown Bay City. When I felt unsteady, I would jump to the other rail without falling off to regain my balance. On Mom's $20 allowance day, I could always bum a quarter off of her and head downtown for a pack of cupcakes and a quart of chocolate milk. Cupcakes were 5 cents and milk was 18 cents, so I had 2 cents left over for penny candy. Sometimes Mom sent me to the store to buy her feminine products, which I hated to do, so she always paid me a quarter.

There was a trestle about 2 blocks north of our house (on the way downtown) that we could play on. Under the trestle was a very slow-moving creek where you could find water dogs (5-inch to 6-inch lizards, dark brown with bright yellow on one side, that were safe and fun to play with). A speeder could be heard coming from a mile away, alerting us so we could leave the area or hide, to avoid trouble with the railroad employees for being on their property.

Before 6th grade, my dad picked out the usual two pairs of socks, two flannel shirts, two pairs of jeans and one pair of cheap shoes for my brother Billy and me. We were never consulted about any school clothing purchased, and my mom never went to the J. C. Penney store with us. The store had a neat vacuum system way to pay your bill (no other store I was ever in had one). The sales clerk put a copy of your purchase and payment into a capsule 2 inches in diameter and 6 inches long and dropped into a vacuum tube that went very fast to the only person in the store that accepted money for a purchase. This person kept a copy of the receipt and placed your change in the tube and sent it back to the area of the store you and your sales clerk were in. The cashier was located above the floor that displayed items for sale, called the mezzanine. As always, the new clothes had to last until the start of the next school year.

I made friends with a Tillamook Boy whose dad worked on a mill pond at a sawmill at the east end of town on East 3rd Street. We visited his dad at work because my new friend wanted to show me how the log trucks drove up to a landing and a large forklift pushed the logs off the truck and into the water, causing an enormous splash. My friend's dad walked on a log raft wearing calk boots to grip the logs and used a pike pole 20 feet long to push the logs into position to go up the chute and into the saw blades.

I had on my new school clothing, including new shoes, and his dad allowed both of us to walk on the floating log raft. I walked on a log that was not secured to the other ones and it started to spin. The log rolled faster and faster until I could no longer maintain my balance, so I fell into the water in my new school clothes. I went down about 10 feet below the waterline into very dirty water and saw bark floating underwater everywhere. My friend's dad pulled me out of the water with his pike pole. I never told my mom or dad what happened.

One time we found a pet goldfish over 7 inches long that somebody had released. It was in a water-filled ditch 4 feet deep beside Hwy 101, two city blocks north of our house. The fish had an enormous belly the size of my fist. Not wanting to harm an animal, I just watched it swim.

The railroad was owned by Southern Pacific Company, with a branch office on East 5th Street in Tillamook and one in Garibaldi with both freight and passenger service. Bay City was a larger city in earlier years with a large, 4-story hospital (the 6' foundation walls still stand in place, covered by berry vines and other brush). A tall hotel overlooked the Bay just below the hospital that was on Portland street, one block east of Highway 101. The 3-story hotel was called The Bayview and was just a few feet from the Bay.

There was also a broom factory and a beauty shop in Bay City. The town also had a passenger train depot and a dock for boarding boats to go to Bay Ocean on the other side of the Bay. An Annual Oyster Festival took place in Bay City, where long holes were dug that held hot embers for cooking the oysters in their shells and sold. While I was growing up, this happened every year beside Highway 101 near Hayes Oyster Ave. There was also an auto court (an older name for a motel) called The Blue Top Auto Court, a basket factory, a builder's supply company, and an electric plant with a tall smokestack.

My dad continued to work on our one-room house, adding more rooms every month while working on both of his days off from his regular job at Buel's Hardware. He also worked every night after dinner until late in the night. My dad never asked me to help him build our new house, thinking I was too young in 1946. Later on, in the 7th and 8th grade, he asked if I would help him build two houses that he built and sold on the G.I. Bill. We built one house on our property, on a lot on the far southeast end, and sold to Mr. Art Tucker. Mr. Tucker bought the house using his G.I. Bill loan. Mr. Tucker later sold it to Bill and Janet Lane, who were related to him (Tucker was Bill Lane's uncle). The other house Dad and I built was four blocks down our gravel road on the south side, on a lot Dad had purchased. Dad and I built these two homes on his days off from his clerk job.

Later in life, I helped Dad build an apartment on his property between his house and the Tucker's house. The apartment had two 2-bedroom residences and one 3-bedroom residence that Dad planned on renting and later selling for a retirement fund.

The Bayview Hotel, Bay City, Oregon.

Bay City Hospital.

Bay City Basket Factory.

Downtown Bay City.

I decided to explore our new property, which was about 5 acres of brush behind our house to the west. I had to climb over the top of a large log pile that reached the entire width of the property. The logs had been cut years prior when a city park was clear-cut to make way for homes. The cleared property Dad was building on was about one acre. I found that salmonberries mainly covered the back of our property. These orange colored berries could be eaten, but I thought they had a funny taste. There were also hundreds of red huckleberries that tasted very good. I decided I could not make much money picking and selling them as they were small (about the size of raisins). I found one bush of blue huckleberries. The bush was the only blue huckleberries I ever saw in Tillamook County. I also found an old wooden nail keg about 3 feet tall which appeared to hold about fifty railroad spikes used to fasten the railroad rails to the cross-ties. I reached into the keg to pull a spike out and felt pain in 3 fingers. I lifted my hand out of the keg and found a chipmunk hanging by his mouth from my fingers. I let out a yell, and the chipmunk let go, jumped to the ground, and ran away. The chipmunk did not break the skin on my fingers, so I did not need medical treatment. A couple of years later, I wished I had captured the chipmunk and turned him into a pet. One of my classmates had a pet chipmunk with a one and a half foot yarn tied around his neck and the other end pinned to his shirt pocket. The chipmunk attended school classes with us and also did a lot of sleeping in the shirt pocket.

The following day, I took my fishing throw line with me to visit downtown Bay City because I had seen a small creek passing through the city that came from Doughty Mountain several miles to the east and ran into Tillamook Bay. The creek was located two blocks north of Brownie's Tavern and one block west of what was then Highway 101. The creek is about 6 to 8 feet wide and 6 inches to 24 inches deep and was full of small trout. I baited my hook with a single red salmon egg. My throw line had a small split shot sinker on it. I caught four trout. Three of the trout were cutthroat and one was a rainbow. All of them were 6 inches to 11 inches in length. I loved this city. Where else could you sit at the edge of a city street, two blocks from city center, dangling your legs over a culvert that allows a creek to pass under the street and catch a limit of trout?

My best income as a child came from Alderbrook Golf Club, located about one and a half miles south of Bay City on old Highway 101. Billy and I walked to the course more than 300 times over the years. We usually stopped in Idaville at Don Rinkers' small store on the way to and from the golf course. It had a fine assortment of candy and other items we wanted.

Babe and Alice True ran the 9-hole course with a clubhouse where golfers could rent clubs for 25 cents in a golf bag. There was a #2, #5, #7, and a #9 iron with a driver and spoon or Brassie woods. There was also a putter in every bag. The rules for golf ball hunters were do not speak to players and do not try to sell golf balls to players or they would ban you from the golf course. There were two water hazards (small lakes) on #5 and #7 holes. The water was only about 3 feet deep. We would roll up our pants and wade out to pick up balls from the water in plain sight and would feel around in the soft mud for other balls. The lake balls were less desirable as most golfers used older cut-up balls in case the ball didn't clear the water. I did not subscribe to this idea and used my good balls on the lake holes when I played golf. Why go to a hole with a negative attitude?

The lake balls would only bring us about 10 cents each. The other better balls that were sold to Babe True at the clubhouse at the end of our hunt brought 25 to 50 cents each. We could earn $5 to $6 per hunting day. The club stamped your name on all your balls if you were a club member for a stamping fee. When the stamped balls were found, the finder received 10 cents per ball, and the owner paid 10 cents for the found ball. Hunting balls was fun, just like hunting Easter eggs. Hole #3 was a large hill about a city block tall. Some golfers reached the top with one stroke. The golfers could not see their ball land on the top of the hill so it would be easy to hide out in the trees behind the green and swipe the balls, but we never did. Hole #2 was beside a swamp filled with skunk cabbage where we found many golf balls among the weeds and the water dogs (lizards) that were harmless but kept a lot of lady golfers from looking for their lost balls.

My brother Billy and I also found many garter snakes while hunting for golf balls. Some snakes had a red stripe down their backs so we called them 'red racers.' Some had stripes that were yellow, blue, or green. The snakes were harmless. I do not think they even had teeth. We didn't bother them, and they didn't bother us. We used to see three to four snakes a day.

I haven't seen a snake in years because people have killed a lot of them off by using poison on their lawns and other plants. We also used to see over 12 bumblebees per day and five times as many birds and honeybees.

There was no money to be made being a golf caddie, as the course did not encourage this idea. Every morning and evening, dairy cows would hold up play as they walked across the fairway on holes #9 and #1, going from pasture to the barn and back again.

A teen boy's golf tournament was held when I was sixteen. They expect-ed me to win due to all my experience playing golf. It was reported that Skip McVey and I were tied for the win going into the last hole. On my second shot, the ball slammed into a very tall fir tree that grew in the center of the fairway and returned behind me, over my head. This cost me a stroke and I lost to Skip by one stroke coming in second place with no trophy.

One time, I was hitchhiking to Tillamook from Bay City to go to a movie with money earned at the golf course. A man picked me up and said he was on his way to work a swing shift at Oceanside Lumber Com-pany. The man kept passing a bottle of whiskey to me and I would take a good, long drink. I got out of his car in Tillamook, and he continued on to operate a lumber mill saw half drunk.

6th Grade
1947 - 1948

I entered the 6th grade on September 5, 1947. Mrs. Goldie Fogg, who taught 5th and 6th grade, was still my teacher and she was a good one. Everyone liked her because she treated everyone fairly and was like a second mom to all of her students. She was in her 50s.

The Bay City Water Department headed up by Joe Flisram and another employee dug a trench down our street near our front yard and installed water pipes around this time. Dad worked fast to add a bathroom sink, tub with no shower, and a commode to our bathroom. We had to enter the bathroom by passing through Mom and Dad's bedroom, which us kids tried not to do too often and never at night. Dad removed the outhouse and filled in the hole after two years of use. A large hole behind the bathroom had to be dug and a septic tank installed. Once a year, a large tank truck came and pumped out the septic tank. Bay City had no sewage plant at that time.

Joe Flisram was also the Bay City cop and wore his badge while doing his water department job. He drove an unmarked city pickup. I never heard of him doing any police duties, including writing tickets or making arrests, but Bay City kids still avoided him.

Dad continued to remove large fir tree stumps from our front, side, and backyard. This process lasted until about 1960. He had an 18-inch cylinder-shaped wedge, 3 inches in diameter that he drove into the stump, unscrewed the wedge cap top and poured in black powder, added a fuse and would blow up or split the stumps. There was a stump by our driveway near the city gravel road that was 10 feet tall and over 4 feet in diameter, with holes cut by an ax in the side of it for climbing. I used to sit on top of this stump and watch people and cars pass by. Another interesting stump sat near our driveway, but closer to our garage. This stump was rotten inside, 3 feet tall, 3 feet in diameter, and hatched hundreds of flying termites every Spring.

I walked by myself to the Bay City Methodist Church every Sunday since Dad was an Atheist and Mom, who believed, was more or less housebound. I looked forward to going. I didn't have church-going clothing, but nobody cared.

The only time I ever got in trouble in all my school years, other than missing too much school in the seventh and eighth grade, was when I kicked a 7-inch red rubber ball so hard it left the school property and I did not go to get it. Someone told on me, and Mrs. Fogg asked me about it. I told her, "yes, I kicked the ball."

Mrs. Fogg said I could stay after school for a week or I could have a spanking. I told her I will take the spanking, as I had so many of them while growing up. One more was no big thing. Mrs. Fogg never brought the matter up again, and I never got a spanking.

During my entire time living in Tillamook County, our phone never rang for someone to try to sell something or share a political message. There were door to door salespeople instead. I'd guess there were at least three sales people per week at the door, both male and female. The Avon lady, Fuller Brush man, Watkins products, and others came once per month, every month. Other sales people sold an assortment of things. Mom would always be polite and listen to what they had to say and inspect their products. Mom never had any extra money left from her monthly allowance to buy anything. One time, when I was in the 6th grade, Mom bought an Electrolux vacuum cleaner. Why, I do not know. Mom made the purchase with nothing down and $5 per month. The machine cost $59.95 plus a few dollars extra for the monthly payments.

Mom told me and my brother Billy not to tell Dad as she planned to tell him after dinner, when he was in a good mood. I was not present when she told him she had made the purchase. Mom never had a rug in her lifetime. Some of our floors were plywood, and some were linoleum. Mom used a broom and mop to clean the floors, sweeping the debris onto newspaper and putting it in a paper bag we had received from the store. Mom did not have a dustpan. Mom would mop the floor and tell everyone in the house to walk on the newspapers she had laid on her wet floor. There were no plastic bags then. There was no garbage pickup in Bay City at that time. Dad took garbage to our city dump. There were no restrictions on what you could dump and no fees. I do not remember seeing a garbage can in Bay City growing up. In the 1940s, Bay City had to move the city dump from the northwest side of the city to the northeast side because it was too full.

Dad purchased a lot for $100 on Ninth Street, on a hill overlooking the bay, which had a wonderful view. On it was one very tall fir tree that was about 90 feet tall. The lot cost Dad a little less than $20 per year in property tax, and some day he was planning to build a house there. As times were hard and Dad's pay as a store clerk was small, he gave the lot to the county for taxes due. Today the tree alone would bring over $1,000 and the lot between $40,000 and $50,000.

I worked for several weeks, making 50 cents per day, feeding and caring for several rabbits owned by Nick S., who lived about two blocks down our road towards the bay, when the family went on a vacation trip.

One time, Dad and I stopped to talk with Mr. George R. who had T.B. Mom had a fit telling us to stay away from Mr. R., but he lived two houses down the road from us so he was hard to avoid. At the time and for several years later, persons with active T.B. were locked up in the T.B. hospital in Salem, Oregon and not allowed in public. I used to escort state prison inmates with T.B. to this hospital in the late 1960s.

In the winter of 1947, we had a surprise snowfall of about 3 inches, which was unusual for the Oregon Coast. I was excited about the snow and attempted to ski. Across the highway from our house was a medium-sized hill driveway, belonging to the Bauman family. I went to our garage and constructed a pair of skis out of an old wooden nail keg and was off for a fun day. Once on the hill, my homemade skis were too heavy for the 3 inches of snow and sunk to the gravel driveway going nowhere.

Billy and I used to enjoy walking through Norris' 5 Cent to $1.00 Store after hitchhiking to Tillamook. Skinner's 5 and 10 Cent Store was across the street and posed good competition. One day in Norris' store, when I was 12 and Billy was 10, Billy put a toy car in his pocket. The store clerk observed him take the car and came over and took his arm. I pulled him away from her, saying, "Mom is going to give you a spanking as soon as I get you home." Billy handed the clerk the toy and we headed out the door. The clerk just stood there, saying nothing, as I must have taken her by surprise. Billy had learned a lesson about theft. I had done my big brother thing.

In early June, a heel came off my shoe from normal wear as I walked a lot of miles every year. I found a pair of knee-high rubber boots in our garage, so I wore them to school with my jeans pulled over them to hide them

Norris' 5 Cent to $1.00 Store.

from school staff. This also meant I was barefoot for the summer again until we purchased school clothing in late July or August. The hot, tight boots caused me pain at school because no air was getting to my feet. I ended up getting athlete's foot.

One time, my school friend Eddie and I hitchhiked to Tillamook looking for something to do. We visited my dad at work in the Buel Hardware Store. While I talked to Dad, Eddie walked around the store. Later Eddie and I looked over all the sporting goods and that gave us the urge to go camping. We returned to Bay City to pick up a frying pan for cooking fish, a pot for tea, some tea bags, a can of chicken soup in case we could not catch enough fish for dinner, and 2 blankets. We did not have sleeping bags. We hitchhiked South on Highway 101 about 2 miles and started our 3-mile walk to Kilchis River Park, as there was hardly any traffic on Kilchis River Road to hitchhike further. While walking, Eddie pulled an expensive Shakespeare brand fishing reel out of his pocket and used the screwdriver on his swiss knife to take the reel apart, throwing one piece at a time into the roadside brush, which I thought was strange. I asked him where he got the reel and he said, "I took it from Buel Hardware while you talked to your dad." As we were walking to the park, Eddie told me he had stolen a car and hit a power pole at the corner of Doughty Road and Highway 101. After the accident, the car was a total wreck, and they never caught him. At this point, I decided Eddie was not the kind of person I wanted to be friends with, so when our camping trip was over, so was our friendship.

We arrived at the park and stashed our gear, then we went trout fishing with throw lines, using grubs for bait. We soon caught a pan full of fish for our dinner. After dinner, we still had some daylight left, so we hiked to and walked on a 60-foot rope bridge that is now gone. Before bedtime we had target practice throwing our hatchets at an enormous fir tree. A couple of years later I checked the fir tree out and it still had our hatchet scars, with a lot of dry pitch covering the wounds. I felt a little bit bad for the tree. This trip was the last thing Eddie and I did together. The following year, he moved from Bay City to Seattle, Washington.

7th Grade
1948 ~ 1949

I passed the 6th grade with high marks and started the 7th grade in September 1948. A teacher taught the 7th grade and 8th grades (name withheld) who was a joke. This teacher was in the classroom less than half the school day. He must have spent the other four hours in the basement boiler room, smoking or visiting. When he was present, he had no control over the two classes. Students wandered around the room, sat with girls at their desks, or left the classroom. There was also a lot of talking noise in the classroom. I do not remember learning anything in the 7th grade. When the teacher left the classroom, we hid all the chalk and erasers behind the 3' x 3' pictures of Presidents Lincoln and Washington that hung on the wall above the blackboard. The teacher was always looking for chalk and erasers, to no avail.

One day, in the Spring of 1949, we had a 5.0 earthquake, which is rare for Tillamook County. All the chalk and erasers fell to the floor from behind the pictures. The teacher found out where the chalk went. That teacher did not last the school year, and they replaced him with another teacher named Mr. Wally Ramp.

In the spring of 1949 while I was in the 7th grade, I was walking near Bay City Grocery and two girls who were sisters approached me and asked me if I wanted to watch an X-rated film that belonged to their mom and stepdad. The older girl was in the 6th grade and the younger girl was in the 5th. I was not yet interested in girls, so I told them no. Seeing naked men and women would have embarrassed me.

When she was in the ninth grade, classmates found the older sister in the cloakroom (a walk-in closet on the east end of the high school study hall where the students hung their coats and hats). It was a room I never used because I never owned a hat or coat while in school. The girl was crying and when asked by her friends why she was crying, she said, "I want to go on a date with Gordon." Two of her friends came to me and asked me to date her. I agreed to the date so she would stop crying and come out of the closet to do her schoolwork. We went on one date, which turned out to be a car ride in the back seat of my friend's car with a lot of hugging and kissing going on, but not more than that.

Later in life, when I was a Chief of Police in a Washington County city, I crossed paths with the younger sister again. I was woken up at 3 a.m. by one of my on-duty officers who had the girl in custody for being drunk and sleeping beside Highway 8. The girl told the officer she was an old friend of mine and asked if she could be driven to my house. The officer agreed to bring her to my house, and I took custody of her. The girl slept with me in my bed with no advances by her or me. The girl left after breakfast and I did not see her again. A week later she was killed just east of Tillamook on Highway 6, after hitting a truck head on.

A man who lived in a clearing in the woods east of our house in Bay City said he was starting a Boy Scout Troop and asked me to join. The man had about 10 kids of his own. He was very poor. They lived in three shacks, one for eating and two for sleeping in. He did odd jobs for a living and had no vehicle.

I hitchhiked with him to Tillamook and we did two or three yardwork jobs together. I was paid $1 per hour. The following week all the boys he had recruited met at his place. We were told our first assignment as Boy Scouts was to build a large garden roughly 50 feet by 100 feet. After working several days for him for free, we decided he was not in any Boy Scout program and just wanted free labor. We all quit and went home. A month later I ran into the man and he asked me if I would let him spank me for $5. I told him yes. I went to the area where he lived and he sat on a stump and he placed me over his knees and pretended that a spanking was on the way. He then said he just wanted to see how brave I was and I could go home with no spanking and his $5. I decided he was a nut and stayed away from him in the future.

When I was in the 7th grade, my brother Billy and friends started fishing off the end of Bay City docks for perch and Tom Cod. We knew where a small stretch of sand was just north of the docks. The rest of the Bay had a mud bottom. We used sand shrimp and kelp worms that only lived in the sand as bait for perch. At high tide, we could catch a whole gunny sack full of 5-inch-wide and 7-8-inch-long perch. During a Tom Cod run you did not need any bait, as there were hundreds of fish fighting to get on your shiny hooks. We used 3 to 5 hooks at a time and caught 3 to 5 fish at a time. Tom Cod were about 6 inches long and shaped like freshwater trout.

The dock had fish and crab companies like Tillamook Fish and Crab, Gage Fish Company and others in large buildings on the west end of the dock. There was an open area with a protective rail that we would fish off on the far end of the dock, about a city block out from the bay's bank. One time, while we were fishing, our friend LeRoy pushed my brother Billy in the back, knocking him off the dock. Billy had about a 20-feet fall into 8 feet of water. A worker at Gage Fishing Company heard the yelling and came to the rescue with a long pole and fished Billy out of the Bay. Le-Roy was asked why he would push somebody into the water. He replied, "I thought it would be funny." Then LeRoy headed for home instead of getting beat up.

Mr. Normo, who owned Bay City Grocery, had a stepson named John, who was about 4 or 5 years older than me. John was a big kid. He was 6'7", 230 lbs. He became a good friend. One time, John carried me on his shoulders from Bay City to Larson's Cove, a trip 1 ½ miles north along a clay bank above the railroad tracks. I was able to pay John back in 1952. John went into the Army and was killed in Germany in a Jeep rollover accident. I had joined the National Guard and was part of Company M, so I volunteered as a pallbearer when Mr. Normo requested a military funeral. John had carried me, so now I carried him. We laid John to rest in the (IOOF) Oddfellows Cemetery in Bay City that is also the place where my mother was buried.

In 2015, I tried to find John's grave, to no avail. His grave was at the top of the hill, near an enormous tree. Maybe his last name was not Normo because he was a stepson. I checked with the graveyard's current owner and we could not find a record of John—there was no marker.

Prior to school's start, I went fishing in Doughty creek on the mountain by myself. I camped out by myself for a couple of nights. There were so many fish and they were so hungry that they bit on just shiny hooks with no bait.

John B. "Jack" Ross

*John's last name was Ross. The name on his grave was Jack B Ross, and in the
cemetery registry we found him in it was John B "Jack" Ross.
We were able to find his real name using census records.*

8th Grade
1949 - 1950

On my first day of 8th grade, while playing basketball in the indoor gym, I noticed two new young teachers, one of which was Mary M. from Grants Pass, Oregon, who would be my 9th-grade Biology teacher. I was told that she was 21 years old. Miss Mary M. drove a 1948 Ford and lived with a local family.

I started the 8th grade in September 1949. That year, Dad also ordered a telephone to be installed. Our phone number was 390. He ordered a phone on a four-party line because it was about 75% cheaper than a private line. This meant the phone rang for 4 households. Each household had a ring from one to four rings, which consisted of a mix of long or short rings. Our ring was 3 short rings. This meant if any of the other households received a phone call, it would ring in everyone's house. There were a lot of printed directions on how to use a party line. Most of the time when you picked up the phone to make a call, someone else was talking on your phone, so you had to wait. Private lines could be purchased for about three times the fee. Years later, our phone number changed to DR7-2314. When the Tillamook County phone system outgrew the three-number system, it was replaced by one word like Drake (a male duck) and five numbers. Only the first two letters of words used were dialed—DR for Drake.

The Telephone company in Tillamook County was the Pacific Telephone and Telegram Company, except for Cloverdale and DeLake, who were served by Tri-County Company and Nehalem Telephone and Telegraph Company served Nehalem. In 1936, Bay City had 27 listings. The phone number for the phone company was 4. There were three fish companies—Gage Fish's phone number was 232 and Tillamook Bay Fish Company's phone number was 363. No grade school is listed, but the high school was 63. No fire or police numbers were listed. To call Tillamook Fire Department, you'd dial 77. By 1947, Bay City had 87 listings. Tillamook listed two taxi cab services

– Don's Cab and Deluxe Taxi—phone number 6, whose stand was located in the Tillamook Hotel. The 1947 phonebook lists four different rates to out-of-town points that depended on the time of day and the day of the week a call was made. The call to Bay City from Tillamook was 5 cents. The call fee to Garibaldi was 10 cents, to Los Angeles was $1.65 and to Salem was 40 cents. The 1952 phone book has all kinds of good tips in large print words throughout the book, such as Telephone Courtesy—Win Friends—Answer Promptly—Speak Pleasantly and hang up quietly. Another quarter page statement reads, 'Please listen for the dial tone—turn the dial all the way and then let it go back naturally without forcing. Answer promptly, the person calling may decide that no one is there and will hang up.'

Another notice reads, 'Memory plays tricks. If you are in doubt about a telephone number—look it up.' For your time of day, call the operator. A full-page ad shows how to use a party line— 'Space your calls. Hang up if your party line neighbor says they have an emergency. Always make sure the line is clear before you dial for a call and replace the telephone carefully after you complete your call.' Some early phone books listed your address following your name.

In the early 1970s, a Eugene, Oregon company issued a directory of citizens of Tillamook County that was sold by subscription only. The directory included alphabetical listings of businesses, private citizen, and miscellaneous information about the cities and the county. Federal, state, county, and city officials were listed. The directory listed the citizen's address, phone number, occupation, spouse's name and all the children's names who still lived at home. There was also a business yellow page section. The directories were 'must have' books for many businesses and citizens alike.

I learned to roller skate when I was 14, using money earned hunting golf balls. A Frenchman named Perry leased the building from the Tillamook County Fair Board on the fairgrounds about ¾ of a mile east of Tillamook on 3rd Street. Skating was cheap and we could rent skates for 25 cents. Perry enjoyed kids and took us in his car to Rockaway Swim Natatorium often.

Perry was an excellent swimmer. The natatorium drew saltwater out of the ocean through a 4-foot diameter pipe that extended over the beach and into the ocean. They then heated the water. The 'Nat' is gone now, but used to sit where the large downtown parking lot is now. The 'Nat' building also had a 6-lane bowling alley above the swimming pool and a neat penny arcade half a block to the South. Skating was open at the fairgrounds from 7 p.m.

to 10 p.m. on Wednesday, Friday, and Saturday with skating also on Sunday afternoons. It was good clean fun and a good place to meet girls.

I came across Herb Miller on the Kilchis River one day and he invited me to go along with him. Herb wanted to show me how to set animal traps. He was after mink and muskrats. Herb made his living trapping. He walked to Bay City, Oregon from Polk County, Oregon behind his dad's covered wagon long ago. Herb's dad was a doctor who worked at the Bay City Hospital. Herb lived with his Native American wife off of Doughty Road in a cabin with hides, horns, and pelts nailed to the walls. They had an outhouse, no electric service, and no running water. He invited me to visit his cabin and meet his full-blooded Native American wife, which I did a few days later.

After learning to trap from Herb, I ordered 6 traps from Sears Mail Order Company. I went trapping on Doughty Mountain. I checked my traps the next day and found that I had caught a skunk. I was so proud; I took it home in a gunny sack across my back. Mom had a fit, and I had a bath. I'm now sorry for the skunk's life I took for no good reason. I gave up trapping.

My friend Jerry W. has a twin brother named Larry. Larry failed a grade, so was one grade behind us. Jerry and I worked out hand signals for each letter of the alphabet so we could talk to each other in class without sound and no one could understand what we said. To this day, I can run the alphabet with my hands and fingers.

I do not remember what the problem was but once Larry wanted to fight me so we set a time for the fight at 12:30 p.m. behind the school gym. Word spread to other students, so we drew a large crowd, but no school staff members showed up. Larry came towards me, so I jumped on him and put him in a chokehold. Larry gave up, so I let him go. I never had a problem with him again. While serving in the USMC, I came upon Larry in a Navy uniform on Market Street, in Honolulu, Hawaii. We visited and had a good laugh about our fight.

I decided it was time to start smoking. I tried a stalk of dry grass that had a hollow stem. It was very strong smoke and very hot so I had enough of that. More people smoked than not, so cigarette butts were thrown everywhere. I could walk along Highway 101 and find a butt that someone discarded out of a car window about every 20 feet. I would pull off the filter, if it had one, to avoid putting something in my mouth that had been in someone else's mouth. The butts I found with no filter were reused by taking off the burned end and smoking the butt from the end that had been lit.

At age 14, I bought Lucky Strikes anywhere with no questions asked and I was allowed to smoke at home. Cigarettes were 17 cents per pack and $1.50 per carton of 10 packs. Cigarette packs that were sold inside cigarette vending machines had 3 cents on the side under the sealed cellophane because it took two dimes to operate the machine. I would keep an eye out for discarded packages to see if someone had forgotten to remove their change. Like others, I wish I had never started smoking but was able to quit in 1969, after 3 attempts to stop over 20 years. I purchased a 21-inch color TV with large payments I could not afford so I would have to spend my cigarette money on it rather than smoke.

There were no rules regarding leaving the school grounds during school hours, so my best friend Jerry and I would leave school during recess and after we ate our lunch in the school dining room to go smoke. We walked about one and a half city blocks west of the school and sat above the city street on a 30-foot-tall dirt bank. We were often late returning to class but were never questioned about it. If we left the school grounds on a Friday, we had no plans to return to school that day. We had things to do, like ride horses, go fishing, or hitchhike somewhere. Often we would meet at a double car garage meant for faculty use (but never used) that was attached to the east side of the school gym, which was a stand-alone building. The large double garage had no doors. Jerry and I enjoyed hanging out and smoking in the garage that was about 50 feet from the city street. We could hang out at dusk and watch 20 to 30 barn swallows fly past the school gym over and over, catching flying insects. After dark we had to cup our hands to hide the lit end of our cigarettes so passing cars could not see that we were on school property after dark.

When I was waiting on Jerry to arrive one evening, I saw a Tillamook ambulance with its overhead red lights on, leaving the small farm about 2 city blocks away. The next day at school I learned that the nice older man named Joe who lived there had been taken to the Tillamook Hospital. Joe was a farmer, about 85 years old, well known by all. That night he tried to commit suicide by tying a rope around his neck and jumping off the hayloft in his barn. He didn't measure his rope correctly, so it was too long, and he fell all the way to the barn's wooden floor. Joe, who was in deep pain, found he was still alive, with a rope around his neck and two legs that were too old and brittle to withstand the fall. The 25 foot or so fall broke both of his legs. I never learned who found him or how he got medical help, and I never saw Joe in Bay City again.

Using my hard-earned money, at age 14, I purchased a .22 Winchester Bolt-Action Rifle for $19.95 from the Sears catalogue. The price of a box of shells was 99 cents. I used this gun to shoot rats after dark by wiring a flashlight onto the bottom of the barrel. I also shot it on the Bay and in the woods for target practice. It was and still is a violation of Oregon Law to shoot any game animal with a .22-caliber firearm.

After I went into the USMC, Dad burned our family name into the stock of the .22 rifle, to help prevent theft, and placed it in the gun rack behind the truck seat over the rear window. Most Tillamook County pickups had guns in rear window gun racks wherever they went. Dad's pickup was later broken into and my rifle was stolen.

One time, for 3 days I had to wear a pink blouse as I didn't have a shirt for school and the blouse was too small for Mom to wear. She hung both of my shirts out to dry, but they got rained on overnight and were dripping wet. I usually had one shirt to wear and one in the wash. This day I had both in the wash. The reason I wore the pink blouse for three days was that I didn't complain to my mom about it, and I waited until one of my dirty shirts was washed. I wasn't ashamed to wear the plain cotton blouse. I made do.

Dad decided we needed a cow, so he built a small barn 20 feet by 20 feet and went to a dairy farm near the Wilson River bridge on Highway 101 and bought our family cow. We named the cow Cherry. Dad would walk 3 blocks down our street to pasture our cow at the Ray Sexton Horse Farm. Dad walked the cow to pasture every morning and then home again for milking and put her in the barn every night. Two years later he cut a path through the brush on the back of our 6 acres to save a 2-block walk as the Sexton property was next to ours. The path was in violation of the Spotted Owl Sighting Directive, but County Officials never contacted him about it. The first year we had the cow I had been told cows kneel down at midnight on Christmas Eve, so I spent half of the night watching for this to happen from a short distance away. Nothing happened except that I got very cold and wasted half of a night.

Mrs. Sexton, who lived to ride her horses, turned out to be a good friend. Mrs. Sexton showed me how to saddle up, and also how to care for horses. She assigned a small gray mare to me that was named Mouse. I rode Mouse lots of times for many miles. We rode on back roads and also up the Kilchis River. On Saturday night we rode to the drive-in movie near Idaville at dusk, paid admission, removed the saddles, tied our horses to the meter posts that held the speakers and laid on our saddle and saddle blanket to watch the movie. As time went by, I was allowed to get Mouse from pasture and go on horseback rides by myself. One time at the top of the hill, about one mile east of the school, Mouse threw her bit, at which time I had no control. Mouse ran downhill at a full gallop, with me holding on for dear life. Mouse came to a dead stop behind the school building. I thought I would fall off onto the gravel street. She ran for over a mile.

While in the 8th grade, my friend Joe and I decided to liven up Halloween because Halloween in Bay City was pretty dull. The city was quite large in area, but had a small population of 390 people. With the national average of 3 people per household, there were only about 130 houses in all of Bay City. With the city's sizeable area, which only contained about 130 houses, they were about a city block or more apart, except on the hillside just above the schoolhouse. This made for a long walk if you were trick or treating. The older kids who were in high school and had cars spent Halloween in Tillamook where there were more things going on. There were never any activities planned for Bay City kids by the city, the school, or the lodges.

Joe and I decided we would not do anything destructive, but the plan was for both of us to make two tricks each. Our first idea was to change the light bulbs from white to orange that lit up the big 'G' on the hill behind Garibaldi, but we decided that one idea would take up most of the night.

My first new trick was to get a paper grocery bag and line it inside with wax paper to make it waterproof (there were no plastic bags in stores yet), fill the paper bag a third of the way full of fresh cow manure, twist the top of the bag into a giant wick, place it on a sidewalk leading to a house and light the top of the bag on fire, using my Zippo cigarette lighter, while Joe knocked on the front door. My hope was that the resident would run to the burning bag and stomp the fire out.

My second trick involved making a slingshot. I cut a small fir tree branch for the handle and attached two strips of rubber from an old automobile tire inner tube (tubeless tires were not being sold yet. Back then, the price of a good tire was about $28 and new tubes were about $4). Using fishing line, I tied a piece of leather to the rubber strips for the pouch. The leather I used was from an old shoe tongue. My homemade slingshot worked great. I didn't have a plan for using the slingshot, but thought something would turn up that wasn't destructive. On Halloween evening Joe came by my house and we headed out. At my street's intersection with Highway 101, we stopped under the bright street light to look at my homemade slingshot and the bag of cow manure. Before we left this spot, I decided to show Joe how great my slingshot worked. I picked up a small rock, aimed at the streetlight that was a good 30 feet in the air, not expecting to hit it, and the rock hit the steel shade above the bulb and bounced back into the bulb causing a flash of fire and then some smoke. Right off, I knew this was a dumb thing to do because this was my favorite place to stand while hitchhiking after dark. The area was well lit and had a good place for cars to pull off the road. The light was replaced two weeks later, on a new pole about 40 feet off the ground.

Next, Joe and I walked towards the schoolhouse to try the bag trick near there. I didn't want to carry the bag much further than that because of the stench. We found what we thought was the right house, lit the bag on fire, knocked on the door and ran. One thing I didn't plan on was with all the running, we couldn't see the end result. And there was a lot of work involved in setting this trick up not to see the end result. We ran to the school, where Joe tossed some eggs. While at the school, we decided to go to Tillamook to trick or treat. Joe's other planned trick involved a bar of soap, but we didn't end up doing it. We walked to Joe's house, got his old DeSoto and drove to Tillamook. Joe was a couple of years older than me and had his driver's license. Joe and I got quite a bit of candy trick-or-treating in Tillamook.

Neither Joe nor I had a Halloween mask. They sold masks at dime stores for ten cents each. They made masks from mesh fiber material with a rubber band that fit behind your head to hold it on. Masks depicted black cats, clowns, doll faces, jack-o'-lanterns and so on. I never had a Halloween mask while growing up. The most common candy handed out were 3 cent candy bars that were about half the size of the regular 5 cent candy bars. At about 11 p.m., a police car came down the street and a police officer took us into custody for curfew violation. Curfew for children under 18 years old was 10 p.m. on school nights and midnight on weekends. The police officer didn't ask for any identification before taking us to the police station. The officer unlocked the door to the police station and Joe entered the office. The officer then motioned for me to go inside and I said, "After you." The officer went through the door and I ran six blocks north to the city limits and then hitchhiked home. Joe refused to tell the officer my name. I was never approached regarding the incident. The Tillamook officer turned out to be the Chief of Police, who should have been better trained. We had spiced Halloween up.

Leslie 'Skip' McVey and I were asked to be on the high school basketball team while in the 8th grade because there weren't enough students in high school to make the A and B teams. This was the turning point for me to hanging out with older students. My jersey number was 12. I was a skillful player and on the starting team on the 'B' squad. I felt bad because after four years, my mom and dad never came to a game.

The Bay City News Reporter for the Headlight Herald called Mom every Monday to find out if she had any news for the paper. It was hard to believe, but Mom had something to offer every week, even though she was housebound.

Just down a small hill behind the Bay City School Building was an unimproved field that three years later would be renovated into the Bay City High School football field. The field had a baseball backstop on the northwest corner, but nothing else. A young adult named Bill Bailey who had attended Bay City High School and loved the game of baseball gained permission to use the school grounds after hours. He taught the game to the Bay City students on a volunteer basis. I wanted to learn the game, so I joined Bill Bailey and about 20 others after school. Bill was an excellent player and a great baseball teacher. As far as I know we were the only team in Tillamook County. The County was all about basketball. After our practice, we would choose up sides and play a game. I was learning to play 2nd base. Bill Bailey only taught baseball for one year.

Meanwhile, at home, Mom would serve green peas at least once per week. I do not understand why she did, because each time it caused a big commotion at the dinner table. Billy refused to eat green peas and Dad yelled at him and made him sit there until his peas were gone. Billy would try to hide his peas. Finally, an agreement was reached after months of problems at the table. They allowed Billy to take the skin off of every pea and place the skins in a neat pile, only eating the insides of each pea.

From October until July (when the wild game got freezer burned and had to be discarded), we had deer and elk meat every night. From July until October, we had wild duck or salmon nearly every meal except the occasional beef hamburger that was 39 cents a pound or 3 lbs. for a $1. One or two times per month we had oyster stew, which Dad would make because Mom was afraid that she would curdle the milk when she added the oysters. Dad also did all the cooking that involved the pressure cooker because Mom was afraid of the steam noise. A gauge was mounted on top of it for safety, to help the user know to regulate the amount of steam inside.

My friend Jerry H. (Jerald) and I used to ride his 18-inch Doodle Bug scooter (a small lawnmower, gas engine vehicle) to Oceanside and back home at night after going roller skating on a very small rink floor with posts holding up a second floor that the skaters had to dodge. When we rode the Doodle Bug, we had to pull off the road when cars came as we had no lights or drivers' licenses. Jerry H. turned out to be my best friend ever.

Jerry lived with his dad and two older brothers on a very large dairy farm on the east side of Bay City in the Coast Range Foothills. His mother had remarried and lived half-a-mile north of Tillamook, on the west side of Highway 101. Jerry lived in a large, two-story farmhouse. He and I were together day and night from the 8th grade on. We would skip school and walk to Larson Cove to pick up cockle clams laying on the sand at low tide (one of only 3 places in Tillamook Bay with sand instead of mud). We would build a fire from driftwood that sometimes burned with blue and green flames because of chemicals from the ocean water. Then we'd cut roasting poles, cook our clams over the bonfire, and enjoy. One time we found a copper whiskey still on a creek that flowed into Larson Cove on Tillamook Bay. We also spent a full day at the tidewater of Kilchis River, borrow someone's skiff (a small oar boat), float the river down to the bay, and then back to return the boat. We would go camping on Doughty Mountain for two or three days. We kept a hidden stash in a covered hole inside an abandoned pole barn. In the hole were pots, pans, cans of soup, tea bags, a knife, forks, spoons, matches, etc. We slept beside a fire with a blanket for each of us. The fire also kept wild animals away. At night, we could see their eyes shine at the timbers' edge at our campsite. Sometimes there were over ten sets of eyes. At times like this, we did not care about missing school. We also hitchhiked to Jerry's mothers' house every week. We would have 2 or 3 Lucky Lager beers and smoke her Old Gold cigarettes she stored in her bedroom closet. We would spend the entire school day at Jerry's mom's and then hitchhike home. I had to take a signed note to school every time I did not attend. Mom always gave me a note without questions when I missed school. Mr. Leo Hering, the school Principal called Jerry and me into his office together and said, "You two boys will never amount to anything." Years later, after retiring as a Chief of Police, I drove past his house in Bay City, rolled the window down and called out, "I did too amount to something, thank you, Mr. Hering!" He was a great man, just doing his job and doing it well. Mr. Hering told us school records showed we had missed 77 days of school during the 7th

Lucky Lager.

Old Gold Cigarettes.

and 8th grades.

When I graduated from 8th grade, I received a diploma but felt really bad because at graduation I had to wear a pair of my friend Bill's gray tweed pants that were twice as big as I was and his white shirt, which had sleeves that were too long. My friend Bill Lane outweighed me by 100 lbs. I could not wait to get off the stage and go home. For graduation, I received a gift from Mom and Dad, which was a big deal at the time as I had never received any gifts from them. My gift was a very cheap Wyler brand wristwatch that stopped running after two days. Both Jerry and I passed the 8th grade into High School with good grade marks and test scores. Back then, paper diplomas were issued for graduating grade school.

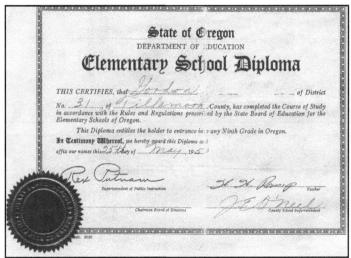

Gordon Lee's Elementary School Diploma.

During the early Summer months, on the third Friday in May, my friend's mother, Iola Lane, decided she was taking me, along with her large family, to Gales Creek to live in a cabin and pick Strawberries. Iola bought all the food, provided transportation and my care out of friendship, never asking for a dime of my picking money. In the evenings, we all swam in Gales Creek behind a small store. We visited a café, listened to a jukebox, ate hamburgers, drank milkshakes, and kept cool. We finished strawberry picking in the middle of June.

In Late June, Dad decided I was going to work the rest of the summer, so unbeknownst to me, he got me a job at a Kilchis River dairy farm as a hired hand about one and a half miles up the Kilchis River from High-

The cafe in Gales Creek that Gordon Lee visited (photographed in 2020).

way 101. Dad drove me to the farm, up Kilchis Road, and dropped me off to live in a small one-bedroom house that was beside the main house, to live by myself for the summer.

While I was packing what few things I owned in a paper bag to take with me to the dairy farm job, my mom came to my room and told me she didn't agree that I should have to leave home at age 14 to work. During our conversation, mom told me that my dad had written a letter to Boys Town, a boys' home in Omaha Nebraska and requested that they take Billy and me as he did not want us anymore. Boys Town wrote back saying they did not take boys who lived at home with their parents. My dad wrote the letter the year before we moved to Tillamook County.

The employer provided meals in the main house. I worked on the dairy farm when I was 14, turning 15 in August that summer. I got Saturday (because it was their church day) and Sunday off except for morning and evening milking. I would have never taken the job if it was my decision because of the long work hours and having to live alone in exchange for small paychecks of $25.00 per month, which was only $.83 cents per day. I could make that amount in an hour hunting golf balls to sell or picking up soda pop bottles along the highway. Child labor laws must have also been violated. I think my dad's reason for getting me the job was to save money not having to buy me food during those months. I did not see my family for the two-and-a-half months I worked there.

A typical day for me that summer was to wake up at 5 a.m. and have breakfast in the main house early in the day so I could assist with the morning milking of their 25 Jersey cows. After milking the cows, I spent about two to three hours cleaning the barn and the Surge milking equipment. We used two Surge milkers to milk the herd. One cow kicked the milker when the machine was installed, so we had to apply kick chains to her back legs to avoid a broken leg from getting kicked. I spent the rest of the day hoeing weeds in the pasture, including rag weed and nettle that burned you if you touched it. The ragweed would make cows sick if they ate it. And it was a violation of Tillamook County law to have any on your property. I also worked in the vegetable garden and chicken house between milkings. I loaded grass hay in the late summer using a pitchfork. The hay was piled on a long wagon and taken to the barn where it was placed in the hayloft, using a large hay hook, ropes and pullies. The hay was fed to the cows during the winter months. The cows were smart enough to come from the pasture to the gate and wait for us to let them into the barn. They also walked to their own assigned stall to be milked. The radio tuned to KTIL was turned on for every milk period to provide music, which had a calming effect on the cows. KTIL was also a good companion for me while cleaning the barn after every milking. Research has proven that cows gave more milk while music was played. After cleaning up from the evening milk period, I returned to my small house and went to bed early after working hard for over 12 hours and having to get up early and start doing it all again. Other than reading, there was not much more for me to do. TV had not come to Oregon yet, and I had no phone or radio. Since I was getting paid $.83 cents a day for the hours worked, and I was working 12-hour days, that meant I was only getting paid close to 7 cents an hour.

The hay needed to lie in the field to dry before being placed in the barn's hayloft. Stacked hay that was green or wet caused heat that could burn a barn down. You had to check the hay by sticking your arm down in it to see how hot it was. Sometimes you'd get hurt if the hay was hot. After the grass hay was dry, we put it in rows with a hay rake pulled by our tractor. It was lots of hard work for 83 cents per day.

One day about a week before school was to start, I left the farm after I saw the owner pulling a calf on a 30-foot rope tied to his tractor. The calf was laying down and being dragged over a gravel driveway, injuring it. This upset me, so I quit the job early. The bawling calf hurt my feelings. I never told anybody why I quit. While working on the farm, I enjoyed attending the auction that took place every Saturday on Highway 101 at Kilchis River Road, in a very large barn. It was a mile and a half walk each way. The auction had household and farm items to bid on. They sold chickens, cows, small calves, and lots of fun things. There was also a snack bar. The chickens would bring about $1 each and some calves sold for $5. Some dairy farms did not want to spend the time or money to raise a calf, so they gave them away for free. Sometimes they were picked up by a rendering plant truck. They gave baby chicks and ducks away for free every spring if you agreed to purchase the food to raise them from the feed store that gave them to you.

One night after the auction was over, I was told by a couple of farmers to be very careful because they sighted a cougar in a field beside the road. My head was on a swivel all the way home. It was a very dark night, so I could not see much of anything.

Bay City High School
1950 - 1953

During the first week of September before high school, my friend Joe H. and I went to Sacramento, California, for the State Fair in Joe's DeSoto. We missed the first week of school. One night on the trip, we slept in the car and when we woke up in the morning; we found the overhead material covered in mosquitos, their bodies filled with our blood. Mosquitos bit us all night from having the windows rolled down for proper air circulation. The worst thing was we had parked in the dark the night before and took out three rows of beans in a farmer's field. The farmer pulled up in his car just as we were leaving and chased us, honking his car horn for several miles down a county road. When we started school one week later, they decided our trip was educational, so they excused us.

I attended the Tillamook County fair by myself that year, on the last day of the fair, which was a Saturday night. I enjoyed looking at the animals and eating at the fair food booths. At 8 p.m. I watched the car destruction derby. After the derby, I attended the carnival on the east end of the fairgrounds. I won a large straw hat with straw fringe sticking out from the brim about 10 inches long.

At midnight, carnival employees started breaking down the rides and clip joint tents. I thought I might find a job, so I contacted the boss and was told the only job still open was to walk the entire carnival grounds and pick up litter with a 4-foot stick that had a nail on the end and a five-gallon bucket. I was told to work the entire night, then contact him to be paid. I walked all night and the carnival area was clean. During the night, the fog came in and you could only see about 25 feet in any direction. The fog ruined my new straw hat, causing it to droop in the moist air. I went to get paid at the boss' trailer, but he was gone. A carnival person had cheated me out of money. I did pick up lots of bottles that I saved for a refund, so all was not lost.

9th Grade
1950 - 1951

Bay City High School was on the second floor on the east end of the school building and took up the entire center of the building. The largest room in the high school was the study hall, where each of the students had their own desk, with each class having their own rows of seats. The 9th grade had three rows of desks on the north side of the room facing west. Next came the 10th grade with three rows of seats, and the 11th grade with two rows, then the 12th grade with one row of seats because there were only 3 kids in the senior class (one girl and two boys). The girl did not attend her graduation as she was told not to because she was pregnant. In those days if a school-aged girl got pregnant she was looked down upon, called awful names, removed from the school system, and in most cases moved to a relative's house out of town.

The east end of the study hall had a typing class area (not enclosed), and a small math room just west of the study hall. Across from the study hall to the west was an English room. The school offices were in the center, and to the east was a biology room. An Algebra room under the gym where Mr. Averill taught math was later made into a shop class. This shop class taught by Mr. Averill was only available during the 1952-1953 school year as the school closed in the summer of 1953.

At the start of the school year, I would go through the empty lockers in the gym to find anything left behind by the rich kids that I could use so I could play sports. Sometimes I found used sweat socks, jocks, tennis shoes or knee pads.

Our English class was a joke. Mrs. D. read a book to us, cover to cover, every class for a year. It was fun to listen to her read the book. It was called The Good Earth by Pearl S. Buck. We didn't learn to spell, about nouns, verbs, or other grammar, nor did we learn any other aspect of English.

Our math class, that was taught by Mr. Hering was great. The typing class that was taught by Mrs. S. was also very good. 15 years later when I was working as a Police Sergeant in Salem, Oregon, this teacher ran over and smashed traffic barricades we were using to block traffic from driving down the city street as we had an electric fire going on a power pole. Some officers were mad and were going to take her to jail. I told them Mrs. S. used to be my school typing teacher and to please let her go on her way. The teacher thanked me and left the area after the handcuffs came off.

Miss Mary M., who I had admired from afar since my first day of 8th grade at Bay City School, was the Biology teacher. Mary M. was a fine looking 22-year-old lady. She had a fun way of teaching, once telling the class she was from Grass Pants, Oregon, rather than Grants Pass. Mary M. paid room and board to live with a family two blocks east of the school, who were friends with my family. She drove her own black 1948 Ford. Mary turned out to be a great friend to me. When I was in the 10th grade, Mary picked me up one evening in her car and the two of us went to Kilchis Park and drank homebrew from quart bottles that my friend 'Hoppy' gave me for free. His uncle, who he lived with, made the homebrew. Mary and I stayed in the park until midnight, drinking beer.

The school still only charged high school kids 15 cents for hot lunches. They furnished all school books with no charge. There were no other school fees, so Dad got by with only paying $30 for school clothing for me and 75 cents per week for lunch. I did not skip school during my high school years, as I knew how important graduation was. I had long hair most of the time due to no haircut money. Our basketball coach would send me home with a note reading, "no haircut so can't play sports." Dad would then give me a dollar, as that was the going rate for haircuts. Little did he know I had found a retired barber with a barber chair in his home that would cut hair for 50 cents. That meant I could hitchhike to Tillamook, get a 50-cent haircut, go to the Saturday afternoon movie for 35 cents, get popcorn for 10 cents and a Coke for 5 cents.

Mr. Eric Fitsimons was the band and choir teacher. Like the other three high school teachers, he taught several other classes including world history, geography, U.S. history, health and physical education. During the 1950-51 school year, the grade school band, which Mr. Fitsimons also taught, had eight members. The high school band had nine members. They combined the two bands to play at most of the school activities, including all home and away basketball games.

Bay City School that was established as District #31 was built in 1920. The school had zero motor vehicles, which meant less tax dollars spent, but it also meant that school staff and students' parents provided all transportation to all activities attended in other cities, including all basketball games. I only rode with Mr. Fitsimons one time as he drove me nuts by playing loud music on his car radio, while keeping time with the music by tapping his foot on the gas pedal making the car jerk faster and slower all the way to Cloverdale for a basketball game. Three or four of the older boys who had evening or weekend jobs owned cars. I never saw a female student drive a car while I attended Bay City School. As a matter of fact, there were far more ladies that did not drive in Bay City, than those who did. Of course, my mom, who was a "shut in" housewife, did not know how to drive during my school years.

The high school boys who owned cars had no rules to follow regarding where to park or the transporting of other students to school activities. During the 1950-51 school year, the high school student body totaled 31 students. 9th grade had 11 students, 10th grade had 7 students, 11th grade had 10 students, and 12th grade had 3 students.

The WW2 blimps remained stationed at the Naval Air Station in Tillamook until I left to join the USMC in October 1953. Flyboys in uniform walked the city streets, which wasn't a problem until I started looking at girls. Many of the flyboys found dates and were resented by the local high school boys for taking the local girls. Blimps from the Tillamook Air Base hangers patrolled the coastline. During WW2, Japanese launched 9,300 Fu-Go incendiary balloons (balloon bombs) which travelled the Jetstream to North America, and some were believed to have caught the Tillamook Burn on fire near the Salmonberry River. That fire started July 9, 1945 and was joined by a second fire on the Wilson River two days later, started by a discarded cigarette. There were also large gun emplacements made with cement in Tillamook County overlooking the ocean. One gun mount is still at Cape Meares Park and Lighthouse, several feet from the ocean on the northside of the entrance road. The Navy stayed at Happy Camp, near Netarts, in the rental cabins and patrolled the coastline on foot with guard dogs as Japanese subs were sighted a short way from the beach there.

A case in point of 'flyboy takes girlfriend' happened to me. I had a steady girl who was in my class the last year I attended Bay City High School. Shirley and I were a couple. When I left for the USMC, we did not have an 'understanding,' so I assumed we were both allowed to date. Shirley wrote to me for about one year, then I did not hear from her again until the 1970s when I learned she had married a flyboy and later divorced with a son at West Point and an ex who was a retired U.S. Air Force Colonel. My payback to the Flyboys walking the streets of Tillamook was wearing my USMC uniform on the streets in many states and overseas, taking the local boys' girls.

My worst day in high school was in math class, which was taught by Mr. Hering. He left the room and Jerry W. and I were having fun flipping a pencil end over end to one another, using our fingers to flip it through the air. We were about 20 feet apart and had gone back and forth for some time when the pencil went right into Jerry's eye. I went home that day after school, not knowing if Jerry was going to lose his eye. His mother called in the evening with the news that the piece of lead was lodged into the white of his eye, the doctor decided that it should be left there for the rest of his life, and he could return to school in a few days after the bandage was removed. What a relief.

One winter day in early December, I found a short white plastic rain jacket that someone lost on the railroad tracks. It was a colder than usual morning in the low 20s. I thought I would wear it on my half-mile walk to school as I did not own a coat. I got outside and pulled on the plastic coat but it was too cold for the plastic; it turned brittle, and the arms pulled off the jacket so I walked to school in my shirt sleeves again. When you own a coat, you never think about it, but when you don't have a coat, that's all you think about.

In 1950, Dad purchased a 21-inch television. There were no shows in color yet. Dad enjoyed having my friends around our house. My house became a hangout. Dad made an enormous bowl of popcorn every night for us high school boys to eat while watching TV. On Friday nights, without fail, was card game night. Dad played with us after we chose partners. We were allowed to smoke in the house after I turned 15. We also drank my friend Hoppy's Uncle's homemade beer. We played cards on the large round mahogany table that Dad made. The TV reception was not the best. We had to use an antenna pointed towards Portland. To set up reception there was a lot of yelling from the person pointing the antenna and moving around on the house roof to someone viewing the TV screen in order to locate the best place to position the antenna. We received channels 2, 6 and 12. The TV went off the air at midnight every night and showed a test pattern for an hour or so before showing static. Channels came back on early each morning.

The early black-and-white TV sets developed problems after being used for a year or so. The tubes in the set would burn out. The most common tubes to go bad were the vertical hold and the horizontal hold tubes, causing the picture to spin up and down or go off the TV screen sideways. To repair it, you could take the TV to a repair shop in Tillamook or repair the set yourself. Some repairmen did house calls, but it wasn't common and was expensive. To repair your own tv, which most people did, you took the back off your set and removed the tubes making a diagram listing the tubes by their number and socket they came from as the TV sets did not have diagrams showing where each tube belonged. Then we had to drive from Bay City to Downtown Tillamook to the Safeway store that had a tube testing machine at the front of the store, along with an assortment of tubes for sale. Each of your tubes, (about six to eight), were placed in the tube tester's appropriate sockets that were marked as to which tubes belonged there. A typical tube number was 6R147 for a vertical hold tube. After the tube to be tested was placed in the tester, a toggle switch was pushed and a needle on a gauge would move. If the needle did not pass the red background area and enter the green area the tube needed to be replaced. The price of new tubes was between $4 and $10 each.

When the color TV sets were first sold the only show in color was The Wonderful World of Disney. A new set of problems came with the new color sets. You could not turn on an electric appliance near your TV set or the colors would run several inches off your picture. The main appliance that caused color problems was a vacuum cleaner. If the colors moved away from where they belonged on your TV screen, it was time to pay a TV repair person to correct the problem because the tool needed to move the colors into the right position was expensive. This tool, used to demagnetize your TV set, was called a degausser and worked like a wand. The cost to fix the color problem ranged from $30 to $50. After paying this fee it wasn't difficult to remember to turn your color TV off before using electric appliances near it again.

Just about every household had a TV viewing light on top of their TV sets, as they believed that watching TV in a dark room would ruin your eyes. Children were also told by their parents not to watch TV while too close to the sets or not to watch for too long because they would ruin their eyes.

Gordon Sr. standing in front of the house in Bay City, 1951.

Friday card game night.

To get your TV set ready for viewing was not as easy in Bay City as it was in the Portland area. In Portland, where the three TV stations sent out their signal, all you had to do was purchase a set of TV rabbit ears to get reception. Sometimes, in a poor reception area you could hang a 12 inch by 12-inch sheet of aluminum foil on both of the rabbit ears for a better picture.

In Bay City, you had to get on the roof of your house and nail an antenna base plate to the roof, being careful not to cause a water leak when it rains, and attach your lattice TV cable to the antenna. The price of TV cable was 5 cents per running foot. Next you had to drill a three-quarter-inch hole in your roof or in the side of your house and pull the half inch wide cable into your attic. Then you had to drill a three-quarter-inch hole in the ceiling above your TV set and drop the cable down so it could be attached to your TV set. One person stood on the roof and slowly turned the antenna until the person inside the house was satisfied that it was in the best position for reception.

Considering that the TV station's signals come all the way to Bay City from Portland (a distance of roughly 60 miles), some homes got fair receptions, and some got no reception. The coast range mountains that are over 1500 feet high and lay between Bay City and Portland might have also caused some interference.

The evening news we watched came on every night at 10 p.m. The weather reports were about what had already happened rather than a forecast as the newsmen did not have the forecasting tools that are in place today, such as weather models and space satellites. One time, mom asked dad if he was going to stay up to watch the news to see what the weather would be in the morning because he planned on getting up early to go deer hunting. Dad replied, "No, you just get up early in the morning and stick your arm out of a window and if it comes back in wet, it will probably rain."

A Bay City boy who had just moved to our city told me his family moved from a house located six miles east of Tillamook on Highway 6, and they had no TV reception there. The boy told me his father installed their new antenna on the home's roof but he got zero TV reception. Two of their neighbors came to their home and told them that all the local people got together and paid a professional person to set up a system they all hooked onto and that they could also hook onto the system for a one-time fee of $500. The boy's dad said they could not afford the fee. There was a 60-foot fir tree growing in their yard near the east side of their house, and his dad decided he would climb the tree and attach his antenna near the top of the tree. The boy's mother did not like the idea and risk of going 60 feet up the fir tree but his dad went up anyway. His dad pulled the antenna up to the top of the tree with a rope after explaining to his son how to hook the cable to the TV set. The antenna was turned in every possible direction while they tried to gain reception to no avail. The boy's dad gave up and decided to come down from the treetop, but he developed a fear of falling after looking down from the tree. After half an hour of holding onto the tree with his eyes closed, his wife called up to him, saying she was going to call the fire department to get him down. The man told her "NO! I would be humiliated." The thought of the fire department coming finally gave him the courage to climb down. The antenna was still up in the fir tree when they moved. They tried to pull the cable loose from the antenna to recover some of their loss, but they could not. His dad refused to climb the tree to take his antenna down after that.

Multnomah Fuel Company built its propane gas plant across the street from our house on an empty lot. They constructed a large office building and a very large storage tank with gauges attached. They also installed a railroad spur track about a city block long so propane tank railroad cars could be side-tracked. They emptied these tank cars into the fuel company's tank that sat on a cement slab on each end. The tank was about 100 feet long and 25 feet in diameter. Hoses were attached to the railroad tanks and the gas contents were emptied into the big tank. Multnomah Fuel Company also had three tank trucks that delivered propane to businesses and homes in Tillamook County. The manager, Mr. Ed Schultz, and two drivers turned out to be good friends. The Fuel Company supplied propane to their customers' tanks, which were used for heat, water heaters, gas ranges, and motor vehicle fuel. The company trucks also ran on propane.

The activity across the street gave my mom something new to watch since she was housebound, except for Sunday drives with Dad. Mom would never ride in a car driven by anyone other than Dad. After I got my driver's license in the 9th grade, I would try to get Mom out of the house and to go somewhere with me to no avail. They took their car ride every Sunday. Sometimes my brother and I were told to go with them. Other than the Sunday car rides, Mom never went outside except to hang wet clothing on the line to dry or to put a meal on our patio table for the goat lady to eat. When I went on rides with them, I used to enjoy seeing a pair of white swans floating on the large lake located on Rockaway's north end beside Highway 101 on the east side of the highway. The swans were always there, as they never

Multnomah Fuel Co. matchbook.

migrated. One year, high speed boat races were held on the lake. The swans left the lake and never returned. Years later, after Dad became a builder, he and another builder named Clearence Hall, who lived about one long city block southwest of the Bay City school grounds, worked together and built a standalone restaurant beside Highway 101 next to the southwest corner of the lake. The building still stands there today.

Ninth grade was over, so Jerry H., and I started to plan our summer activities. We decided on picking cherries in West Salem because we heard the job paid good money. We hitchhiked to Salem with our pots, pans, food and other items, finding a job within a few minutes. We were paid by the pound and lived in a free tent city a few feet from the cherry trees. We set up housekeeping and cooked our evening meal on an iron grate that every tent had. Our neighbors' tents were a few feet away from ours. One neighbor we spent nearly every evening with around a campfire was an older man who had his 7-year-old granddaughter living in the tent with him and picking fruit with him all day. It must have been hard on both of them.

We picked cherries 5 days a week for about a month and hitchhiked to Portland to stay in the New Heathman Hotel and eat at the Jolly Joan on Broadway. Our hotel was one block west of Broadway on Park Avenue. On Saturday night, every trip, we attended The Star Burlesque Theater where no questions were asked about our age. The star of the show, whom we saw several times, was later featured in an advertisement in Reno. She was still dancing burlesque in the 1980s. This was a must-see for me. After her show, she came out front and met with the audience. I talked to her and told her I attended many of her shows in the 1950s at The Star Theater in Portland. Her reply was, "My, that was so many years ago. Thank You."

After the month of cherry picking was over, Jerry and I went from Salem to Sweet Home, Oregon to pick black caps that were small berries used to make food dye. We started work the same day we got into town. They issued us 3 lb. buckets that we wore on our belts so both of our hands were free to pick with. We worked the better part of the day picking the tiny black caps. We worked hard and were paid by the pound picked, which was only a dollar and change each. We decided the job was a joke so we quit and decided on a movie before we moved on. The only thing showing was an Opera male star's life story that was not a good movie for kids, but we paid $.75 cents each and went. Jerry tried to talk me into hitchhiking to Napa, California to pick pears because the old man who lived beside our tent at West Salem had told us about picking them. I told Jerry I had done all the fruit picking I wanted to do this summer and that there were two more months left before the 10th grade would start so I was going home.

In 1951, I took the driver's test at the DMV, which was still in their old location back then across the highway from the new cheese factory, and received my driver's license. Before getting my license, I purchased a 1941 Ford convertible at Tillamook Motor Company. I had only watched my dad drive, so didn't know too much about driving. I drove on the back roads to my house where I could, trying to avoid a traffic ticket for not having a driver's license. I parked the car beside Dad's driveway. When I tried to back out to the city street, I couldn't because I thought the gearshift had to be pushed forward to go ahead and backward to back up. I sat in the car and played the radio for several nights before I learned how to back up. After teaching myself how to drive and getting my driver's license, I drove my car to school, after school, to weekend work, and on dates.

Having my own car while still living at home gave me the opportunity to do many interesting things, one of which was to go crab fishing on Netarts Bay. I always took a friend when I went to Netarts to wade in the bay for safety reasons. I also took a galvanized wash tub along, which I filled with bay water and placed on two driftwood logs, as I wasn't allowed to cook crab on my family's property because my dad didn't like the smell of it. We built a fire under the tub between the logs before we started crab fishing so we had boiling water when we came ashore from our crab hunt.

The tide had to be out but turned to incoming as the crabs were in the ocean and entered the bay to feed as soon as enough water covered the sandbars, which are small islands of sand between the deeper channels of saltwater.

About 30 minutes after the tide started in, we walked out about a city block into the bay, which the tide would cover with water after another hour or two. We walked into the incoming water between the sandbars, looking for crabs that were swimming at the bottom of the channels. We had tied gunny sacks onto our belts to leave our hands free and to have a place to put our crabs after we caught them. To catch the crabs, we used a crab rake, which is a rake with a 5-foot handle and three 3-inch tines. In order to catch one, you needed to trap it on its back as it swims by. The crabs always turned over on their backs and grabbed the rake tines with all their legs. After they grabbed the rake, all you had to do was lift the crabs out of the water and put them in the bag. It was rare that the crabs let go of the rake while being lifted out of the water.

After getting our limit of male crabs (it is not legal to take female crabs or under-sized crabs) we waded ashore and cooked them. The limit of Dungeness male crab is 12 per person that measure 5 ¾ inches across the back, not including the points. Male crabs have an elongated flap on their underside. Female crabs have a round flap.

One time we got carried away and didn't pay attention to how fast the incoming water was blocking our way to the shoreline. We were about a city block out in the bay. Although we had to leave our crab rakes and hip boots behind and swim to shore in over 6 feet of water in some spots, we saved our crabs and had a good meal. Hip boots were about $15 and a crab rake was $5. The bottom line was, we had a very good $20 meal. When I first looked towards shore and saw all that water, I was very surprised and also thought it was a long way to swim and we might not make it. I didn't tell my Mom or Dad about my swim for fear they would not allow me to go crabbing again. By the time we had finished eating our crab, our wet clothing was dry, and we headed for home in our stocking feet with our boots floating out to sea.

We had a secret softshell clam bed where we never saw anyone digging. The clam bed was about 50 feet by 50 feet and had geoduck clams in it. I never heard of geoduck clams being located anywhere else in Tillamook County. The clams weighed from one to two pounds each with a tough neck about two feet long, and a large digger on the end of the body. These clams stuck about one inch of their neck above the bay mud at low tide. We found the best way to dig them was for one person to hold their neck and one or two people to dig them out. The clam was two or more feet deep. After getting one clam, our holes were about two feet long, two feet wide, and two or more feet deep. The geoduck limit was two clams per person. The two to three-foot necks had to be ground up before cooking, as they were very tough. They had stretched their necks to twice their normal length when we gripped them and the clams used their strong diggers to try to escape. One time we saw an Oregon State Police officer waiting in his car near the shoreline so he didn't get his feet wet and we had three clams too many, so we each stuck one geoduck in our boot. We were checked, and I asked the officer how many geoducks we were allowed, to see if he knew about them. The officer replied, "Thirty-six, like all bay clams." We had put the wet clams in our boots for no reason. In defense of the officer, he was not the regular person assigned to enforce wildlife laws on a full-time basis.

I went to the YMCA with my friends to swim. After finding out the cost, I couldn't stay, so I walked out and around Tillamook until they were finished. Years later, I was asked for a donation to help the YMCA. I didn't give one because they didn't help me.

About 3 miles south of Bay City, where the Kilchis River Road meets Highway 101, an auction was held every Saturday evening in a large yellow barn in the late 1940s and early 1950s. Across the highway from the auction barn was a very large grade school building, about the size of the Bay City School. Beside the barn, on the north side, was a small mom and pop grocery store. I would hitchhike to the auction, even though I had very little money to spend there. There were always over a hundred people attending the auction. The barn had a very large snack bar. Some people ate their dinner there. It was fun to hear the auctioneer sell various things. Some of the items that sold were furniture, used appliances, tools, clothing, and live animals. I liked to check out the calves and chickens in their pens and cages. Some bull calves did not get any bids because a dairy farm only needed one or two bulls.

My dad attended the auction from time to time. One evening at the auction, Dad bought several guinea hens for $1 each. Dad kept the hens for pets and for a security system because the hens made a loud noise if other animals entered the backyard. The guinea hens had the run of the backyard during the daytime and went into their chicken wire pen to roost at night. The guinea hens foraged for their food in the backyard. The only care the hens needed was for someone to fill their water bowl from time to time and to lock their pen at night to keep them safe.

Picture on the right: *The front entrance of Bay City School in 1951.*

10th Grade
1951-1952

Upon returning to school in 1951, to start the 10th grade, we found that they had installed candy machines in the hallway. They bolted one machine to the wall on the grade school end of the hallway and one on the high school end. The two machines were about 6 inches wide, 4 inches deep, and 3 feet tall. Each machine held Hershey's candy bars, which sold for 10 cents each. I thought it was a bad idea for a school to sell candy bars to students causing sugar highs, tooth decay and bad feelings for those kids who could not afford the candy.

My dad would not give me a dime for candy, so I found a way to rip off a candy bar or two once in a while that wouldn't cause alarm about missing candy. I broke a double edge razor blade in two and using pliers broke one side of the blade just a little longer than a dime is wide. The coin machines had a push in lever with a hole, and the blade was just a little wider than a dime, so the piece of razor blade "humped up" in the center, causing it to remain in the slot when pushed into the machine. I could empty the whole machine if I had wanted to. Every time I pushed the coin lever into the machine, a candy bar dropped out. I only used my razor blade trick 10 or 12 times that school year and never told anyone about it. The machines must have been owned by the school because the school janitor maintained them.

I worked all the time while in high school when not in class, but was not smart enough to buy the things that would do me the most good, like clothing and a toothbrush. Another job I had just after starting the 10th grade was pinsetter at the Tillamook Bowling Alley located on Highway 6 (the old highway), 1 ½ miles east of downtown Tillamook. Jerry H. and I both worked there setting bowling pins. Automatic pinsetters were not in use yet in 1950. They assigned us two lanes each. There were ten lanes. They paid us an amount depending on how many games we set plus a tip from a bowler once in a while. One time a man rolled a half dollar down the lane to me after his game. When a bowler got a strike, we were expected to pick up 3 pins in each hand and then the last 4 pins to load the pin machine and then pull the lever down that set the pins in the proper space. The signal for a re-rack was to place the bowling ball on the floor by the bowler. We worked two to four nights per week and earned about $6 a shift. Jerry and I had to hitchhike to and from work. Jerry also had a 1 ½ mile walk to and from the highway to get home. Later on, after I was out of high school, my dad put in two more lanes as a builder. This addition took the effort of an expert build-er as the hardwood alley floors had to be dead on level. The bowling alley was owned by Curly and Dorothy Cremer who were great people to work for. I also got to bowl a game or so while working at the alley.

In 1951, a full-size regulation football field was built that ran east to west about 200 feet below the school. The school purchased equipment, full uni-forms for all the players, as well as lined and maintained the field. Bay City played all the local Tillamook County schools who had teams, plus Gaston and Verboort, who beat us 77 to 0 in 1952, our first year. Verboort had very large kids on their team. Driving to a football game at Tillamook Catholic School, our team members, Lee Miles and Ray Hughes, were in a terrible car accident on Highway 101, three hundred feet from our house. Mom, who was a nurse's aid before marriage, ran to assist them. She pulled glass from the windshield out of Lee's mouth and covered both with blankets.

Lee died at the scene. They canceled the football game. They hung a plaque on the school gym wall in Lee Mile's memory. Seat belts were not in cars yet. Their car was struck head on and Lee went through the windshield.

In the 10th grade, the girls of Bay City High School Student Body Club voted and put out a newsletter. The vote was about boys. According to the newsletter, they voted me the boy with the best hair, best-looking eyes, and best voice. This tended to give me a big head.

One of our high school 10th grade teachers knew Jerry H. and I rode horses and camped on Doughty Mountain so she asked if we'd go cut a Christmas tree for the study hall to be enjoyed by all the students if she gave us a school day off to go. We rode double on Jerry's horse named Buck. He was a huge buckskin horse about a third bigger than most other horses. We planned to cut a tree, put it on Buck's back and leading Buck, we'd walk home. We started out the next morning with lunch and a keyhole saw in Buck's saddlebag. By 10 a.m. we were halfway up the mountain and tied up Buck to search a patch of small fir trees for the right tree. We cut a Douglas

Bay City Football Team 1952 wearing black helmets.

Gordon Lee 11th Grade - Age 16.

Fir that was 7 feet tall and carried it to where we had tied Buck so we could eat lunch.

Buck was gone! Perhaps a wild animal had spooked him. He had always waited for us. Jerry and I had to carry the tree about 2 ½ miles to his dad's dairy farm. We didn't know if Buck was going to return by himself, or if we were going to spend the next day or two searching Doughty Mountain for him. As we reached the farm, our pace quickened, wondering if Buck was there. We arrived at the house with the 7-foot tree and there stood Buck with a look on his face like, 'Made you guys carry the tree!' The teachers loved our choice of tree and everyone was invited to decorate it. We cut stars out of colored paper and strung popcorn to make garlands.

The high school also celebrated Valentine's Day. Some of the female students made and decorated a large 2-foot square box for the students to put valentines addressed to each other in. On February 14th, they appointed one student postmaster, and they delivered the valentines in the box to students while going desk to desk. Looking back, I can see that this was a poor idea as the popular students received 20 to 30 valentines while the kids with fewer friends got one or two. Although I received a pile of valentines every year, I felt bad for those who only got one or two. School staff should have figured this out!

In April 1951, I joined the Oregon National Guard, Company M, 186th Infantry, 41st Division of Tillamook, Oregon. I was still 15 years old. Mom would just about do anything for me, so when I found out Bill Lane and several other Bay City High School friends, all older than me, were going to join the Army National Guard I wanted to join up as well. I asked Mom to write a letter to Company M telling them I was born at home, which was common at the time. The letter was to say I was born in April 1935 and list my birthdate as 4-5-35. I had talked to the Company 'M' ONG, and they knew I was underage but told me to get a document to keep them from getting in trouble.

I went with my Mom to the Bay City Clerk's office that didn't know the letter wasn't true, and the letter was signed by my mom and notarized by the city clerk. I joined the Army National Guard and was told my enlistment was for 8 years due to wartime (Korea). I was also told if I missed a drill at the Armory every Thursday night or any days of our encampment at Fort Lewis, Washington every June for two weeks, that I would be picked up by MPs and placed in the Regular Army and sent to Korea.

They assigned me to the machine gun platoon. I soon made gun operator of a .30 cal. water-cooled machine gun. Master Sergeant Howard was
our platoon leader. Our company commander was a full-time district judge,
Captain Bohannon. The first summer at camp, I learned atom bomb sur-
vival skills and how to master my machine gun. We went to the 'EM club'
(enlisted club bar) and drank beer on the weekends, throwing our empty
beer bottles at a fireplace, which was the tradition. They transported us on
a train to and from Fort Lewis. I was there the summer of 1952 and 1953.
We also 'pulled liberty' (leave) on the streets of Tacoma. After less than a
year in the ONG, they offered me a job full-time working at the Armory and
driving an Army Jeep to the Portland area, escorting a 2 ½ ton truck used
to pick up supplies. I worked in uniform for over a year, earning full Army
pay and an apartment that I let my friend CPL. Randy Witt use for free as
he had a family. Later in life when I turned 62, I put in for Social Security
and was told the time I worked for the National Guard couldn't be used for
benefits because my birthdate didn't match my social security birthday, and
if I didn't like this decision, I could go to court. Back then it was against
the law to give an incorrect birthdate to the government for the purpose of
joining the military. I transferred to the USMC in October 1953 to get out of
the Army National Guard because going into another branch of the military
was the only way to get a discharge because of the 8 years of service law
during wartime.

   Our school gym was by far the best one on the Oregon Coast, however
it went unused 80% of the time. The girls' basketball team, coached by Miss
Will, and the boys' teams used the gym for practice and for season games
with other schools. The only other use I can remember was the May Day
Festival. Every year they built a stage on the basketball floor and decorated
it with cedar boughs and flowers. They held a vote and 4 girls from the high
school and 4 girls from the grade school were chosen as princesses repre-
senting their class. They elected one girl from the 12th grade Queen. All
the girls elected as princesses in high school were allowed to choose their
escort. I was chosen prince in the 10th grade, to sit with the royal court on
the stage and dance around the Maypole. This time the borrowed suit came
close to fitting. The suit was black with gray pinstripes, and double-breast-
ed, which was out of style. Parents (but not mine) came to the gym for the
May Day Festival. After a flag salute offered by two boy scouts in uniform,

other speeches were made and then the Maypole dance took place. There was a free-standing pole 30 feet tall in the center of the building. Ribbons, 35 feet long and 3 inches wide, whose color matched the dress of the princess holding it, were secured to the top of the pole. The band of 10 to 12 students played music and couples danced around the pole, weaving in and out of one another, making a nice pattern with the ribbons. The Maypole dance turned out well, but we had several hours of practice before the dance. Mr. Bell, who was a professional photographer and took photos for the school annual, also took photos of the May Day Festival.

One day I went to the Dutch Mill Café and saw my best friend Jerry H. with a girl in my favorite booth, and I joined them. When the girl, Connie B., went to the restroom, I asked Jerry about her. He said he did not know much as he had met her just 2 weeks earlier. I told Jerry I liked his girl and asked him if I could also date her if she agreed. Jerry, being the good friend he was to me, said that was okay. Before leaving the Dutch Mill, I asked Connie if she would go to a movie at the Castle Theater with me the following Friday night and she said yes. We went to the movie together, and I sat with my arm around her during the entire movie. My left hand held what I thought was her breast. When the lights came on after the movie was over, I discovered I was holding her left elbow for the entire movie. The next Tillamook girl I met was June B., who was the same age as me. I went steady with her for several months. June's parents liked me and I was allowed to go on several baby-sitting jobs with her after hitchhiking to Tillamook to be with her. The going rate for a babysitter in 1950 was 35 cents per hour. When it came time for me to return home late at night, there were very few cars on Highway 101. Sometimes I would give up trying to get a ride and just jog home. I could run the six miles from Tillamook to Bay City in about an hour or less.

I attended movies at both The Castle and Coliseum Theaters in Tillamook. The Castle wasn't very clean and live rats could be spotted running across the aisle looking for dropped popcorn and other snacks. The Coliseum, on the other hand, was a neat place. You could stand in the very large, clean men's room and watch cars drive along the main street and see both sidewalks looking through open-air slotted wood vents on the front of the building. Saturday afternoon movies were kids' films like Roy Rogers, Hopalong, and others. The theaters also played Movietone World News, such as coverage of WW2. Another thing that the theaters showed was called a serial, which was a 15-minute segment of a horror film, western, or other genre to make you want to come back the following week to see what happened. The Saturday afternoon shows and Saturday midnight shows were 35 cents each. Popcorn was 10 cents and cokes were 5 cents. Movies during regular hours were 60 cents for adults. Sometimes a free dish was given to each ticket holder. There was a different dish each week in hopes that ticket holders would return each week to complete the entire set. The theater also held a free talent show with local kids trying to get a good prize each Saturday before the afternoon children's show. Attached to The Coliseum on the south side was a walk-up window for service to people on the sidewalk owned by Eldee Confectionary. They sold candy, ice cream cones, and other sweet treats.

Once I had a sore on my back, that would not stop bleeding. The coach saw the blood and sent me home with a note reading, "No doctor, no school." So, I was taken to the hospital where a doctor removed a mole and sewed it up. This was the only time I ever saw a doctor or dentist.

Another day, while on the dairy farm where Jerry H. lived, he decided we would drive the Farmall Tractor around the farm. Jerry drove (without much experience) and I stood on a hitch bar on the back of the tractor. After going about three quarters of a mile, still on the dairy farm, Jerry got too close to a steep hill that led down to a deep hole, and he drove off the edge. Both Jerry and I jumped off about halfway down (about 100 feet) into the hole. We weren't hurt, but now the tractor that was still right side up was 200 feet down in a wooded ditch. Jerry and I walked to a neighbor's farm and explained our problem to Bunn Neal, who was the Bay City retired basketball coach. He agreed to return to the farm with a chain and his larger tractor, and he pulled Jerry's tractor up out of the hole. Jerry's father never found out that we drove his tractor into the hole.

Sometime later, Jerry showed up at my house in his older brother Bob's car. Jerry found the keys to both of Bob's cars at his family's house and took the car without permission. I doubt if Jerry had a driver's license at the time. We took off for Tillamook in the car, turning off of Highway 101 on Latimer Road, which was gravel. Jerry lost control of the car about a half-mile up the road, crashed through a 3-strand barbed wire fence, rolled over 3 times and we ended up upside down. The car was totaled. We were uninjured, even though there weren't any seatbelts at the time. We climbed out of the car, ran about 100 feet and hid in tall grass because farmers who

Bay Ocean Natatorium and Dance Hall.

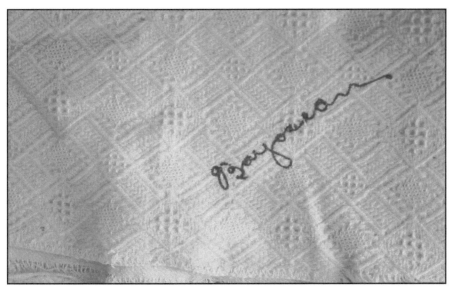

Embroidered Bayocean Hotel blanket.

lived on the road kept stopping to examine the wreck. We finally left the accident scene. Jerry went home and returned to my house the same day as the accident with Bob's second car. We drove to the end of the road I lived on where it meets Tillamook Bay and parked to take a short walk on the Bay. When we returned to the car, Jerry put the car in reverse to back out, but he missed the gear and was not in reverse all the way, which caused a lot of transmission noise and disabled this car as well. Now both of Jerry's brother's cars were destroyed on the same day. I never asked Jerry if he told his family about what happened to both of Bob's cars because I didn't want to put him on the spot.

Ben was another good friend who was in my class, but a year or two older and lived with his single mother and a sister. Ben's mother was a Bay City grade school teacher. Ben was older than his classmates because he had lived with his dad in Alaska in an area that didn't have any schools. Ben used to hang out at my house and played cards with us on most Saturday nights. Ben was keen on firearms and owned several. Ben and I would go to the Bay City dump with flashlights and shoot rats. Rats were all over the dump. Several times we'd have our flashlights off and rats would run across our feet. Ben drove his mother's Nash Metro, a very small car about half the size of a Nash Rambler. We would take his mother's car to Bay Ocean (the city that washed into the ocean because they built a jetty at the entrance to Tillamook Bay). Ben had a movie camera, and we took lots of footage of Bay Ocean before it was gone, including the water pipes sticking several feet into the air.

Bay Ocean was a city bigger than Bay City is now when I first saw it in the early 1940s. I thought it was a fun tourist town, and I also liked the large sign in the picture window facing Tillamook Bay, that read, 'Watch Bay Ocean Grow'. There was a very large swimming natatorium building with warmed ocean saltwater. Bay Ocean had a sightseeing narrow-gauge railroad for tourists and two large hotels. There were many stores, some of which rented crab pots, fishing gear, guns to hunt rabbits, or sold food. On the south end of the area, there was a street with several small houses on both sides and hanging light bulbs. The land developer used these houses as free places to live for prospective buyers while attending meetings put on to sell lots on Bay Ocean. There was no Highway 6 to drive from Portland to Tillamook when they first started selling Bay Ocean lots so the land developer offered free family transportation on Southern Pacific Railroad that

A scene from the Bay Ocean Hotel.

Gordon Lee and the black bear he shot.

brought them to the Bay City Passenger Depot with a steam engine pulling the railroad cars. Then the customers walked a few feet to a boat dock on the bay to board a development company's boat for the final leg of the trip to Bay Ocean. All transportation, to and from Bay Ocean, housing while there and some food was free if you agreed to sit through the property sale pitch. All available lots were plotted and marked with white corner posts. Unfortunately, the entire city washed away into the ocean, gone by the early 1950s, which was mostly blamed on the rock jetty at Barview that changed ocean currents. My friend Ben J. and I filmed what was left at the time with his family's 8mm movie camera. The pictures, which were stored in his mother's basement, got destroyed by dampness. The footage showed streets in piles, with city water pipes standing on end, some of which were 20 feet up in the air. The city's U.S. Post Office was one of the last buildings to be saved. They moved it a mile or so south, and is now a community center.

Many cars were laid to rest and rusted when the ocean washed the only escape road away and the cars had nowhere to go. I have many pictures and postcards of Bay Ocean and also other items, such as a hotel blanket with large letters spelling 'Bay Ocean Hotel'. Ben also played on the Bay City High School football team with me, and his family took 8mm film of our games. The best of the football film I thought was when John H. who played left end caught a pass while playing at Gaston Oregon, in a driving rainstorm and ran sideways about 30 feet to avoid a large mud hole downfield.

Ben was the only boy I knew who always called his mom 'Mother' at all times, which showed a lot of respect. Ben went into the Navy after graduation to work on ocean mines for which he received hazard duty pay. After 20 years in the Navy, he retired and moved to Cornelius, Oregon, where I was Chief of Police. Ben died a few years later, and we laid him to rest in Hillsboro, Oregon.

LeRoy, who pushed brother Billy off the dock for fun, showed up at our house one afternoon and said he ran away from home. We agreed that he would hide in the pile of logs behind our house and I would get some food from our supper and bring it to him. When I arrived to where he was hidden with food in my pockets, LeRoy was nowhere to be found. He had chickened out and returned home. Years later while deer hunting with me in our family hunting Jeep, we saw a doe deer with a very late young spotted fawn down a ridge below the cat road we were on. LeRoy jumped out of the Jeep, saying he was going to shoot the doe because he had a special doe tag. I told him no. She had a fawn that would die without a mother. LeRoy said he didn't care and was going to shoot the doe. I told LeRoy if he shot the doe I would drive off and leave him 20 miles in the Tillamook Burn. LeRoy killed the doe. I sat and watched as LeRoy put the doe on his back and walked uphill towards the Jeep with the little fawn following LeRoy near his feet. The fawn was following his dead mom. I was so mad I left LeRoy and his deer prize in the middle of nowhere. I do not know how LeRoy got home as I never talked to him again.

I shot a black bear in God's Valley just off Kilchis Road, about one mile south of a dairy I worked for on Kilchis Road. It was open season year-round on bears. I intended to cut and freeze the bear meat.

My brother Billy and I were deer hunting and didn't see a buck deer all day. On our way out of the Tillamook Burn, I spotted the black bear walking across a brush free hillside at a fast pace. The bear was only about 300 yards away. I took one shot and missed my moving target, but the bear had stopped walking. My second shot killed the bear. It was a male black bear about 3 years old and weighed 250 lbs. after being field dressed. Billy and I decided to carry the bear and our hunting equipment out in one trip, as it was only about a half mile to the road. We cut the bear in half, which ruined the pelt. The bear had been only one mile from the dairy farm on Kilchis Road, which I'm sure he visited.

My dad decided he'd skin out the bear and hung it in the garage. Halfway through, Dad gave up saying the legs looked too much like a man's legs. I had to finish the job. After we skinned the bear, our family (Dad, Mom, Billy, and I) gathered around the kitchen table to cut and wrap the bear meat. We always processed our meat as a family on the metal table. I was proud to have shot the only bear by a member of our family. Sadly, after cutting and wrapping the bear, the freezer went out and all the meat defrosted and spoiled. After that I wished I hadn't shot the bear! I did see one larger bear while living on the Kilchis Road but didn't shoot it. It had knocked over a garbage can.

While in the 10th grade, Dad obtained his dream job of becoming a carpenter after being a hardware store clerk and working as a mill right (all-around repair person) at the Garibaldi Plywood Mill. A building contractor named Lloyd Sperling hired dad. Dad built hundreds of homes, dairy barns, dog runs and dog houses for the Air Force at Mt. Hebo. He built restrooms on the Garibaldi dock, liquor stores, drugstores, and many more things during his 40-year career as a builder. Dad was fair with his fees, never

GORDON LEE

getting rich. For example, I went on a job with him to the Juno Inn Hill area
to replace the siding on a residence damaged in a big windstorm. The siding
that needed to be replaced was no longer made or sold, so we took a trip to
a lumber store in Tillamook and Dad used their table saw to reproduce the
boards he needed for the job. We returned to the job site and made the home
look as good as new. I asked Dad what he intended to charge for the job and
he said, "Nothing, I did the original work." You can bet the owner of the
home was thrilled. Dad built frozen food lockers for C and W Grocery for
our friend Art Crossley, who went on several deer hunts with us. The lockers
were built where the post office sat that was connected to the south end of
Jack Decker's store, who sold to Art and his partner. Art ran the meat market
and his partner ran the grocery side of the store. Dad also built a very large
smoker on the west side of the building. The smoker is the one that started
Tillamook County Smoker, which is now a large company in Bay City with
several employees and well-known across the U.S.A.

I enjoyed spending time with Leo H., my girlfriend, Shirleys' father, at the
railroad express office where he worked. We would push a large wooden cart
on iron wheels across the railroad station platform to the steam train baggage
car and unload those items transported to Tillamook and take them to the
railroad express office until called for.

I also put new copper plumbing in under my girlfriend's house because Mr. H. could not fit in the space below the subfloor. In 1954 Shirley wrote me a letter while I was in the USMC at El Toro, California, to
let me know her father had died. My day was shot. I felt so bad I wrote
on the fly page of my 3-inch black bible, "I was told today that my best
friend died." I still have the bible.

I spent a week after school collecting money for the March of Dimes. I
went to every house in the Bay City limits and raised a large sum for charity.
I decided on an Oregonian paper route and delivered newspapers door to
door to about 100 customers. I would start work at 5:30 a.m. seven days per
week and then after school another week collecting payment. I entered a contest to see who could get the highest number of new subscribers. I won in the
category for cities the size of Bay City and they awarded me an all-expense
paid trip to Canada. The trip started with a bus ride to Portland on the Oregon Stage Lines. I purchased a very small camera in Portland to use on the
trip. We boarded a bus to Seattle, and once in Seattle we boarded a ship, the
T.E.V. Princess Marguerite, and were assigned staterooms with 6 beds per

Souvenir teacup and saucer from the T.E.V. Princess Margeurite.

Hopalong Cassidy button and coin.

Hopalong Cassidy record,
Hopalong Cassidy and the Square Dance Holdup

room. On the ship trip to Victoria, a kid opened skunk scent used by trappers in our stateroom, forcing us to evacuate the room. The ship's crew were not happy having to deal with this situation.

After arriving in Victoria, they gave us the choice of going on guided tours or going out on our own. Like a fool, I went with some other boys on our own and we ended up at a movie, Willy and Joe, Up Front, a war comedy. Our next stop on the Marguerite was Vancouver Island where some of our group started a very large fire with fireworks on a dock, burning several boats. The fire made front-page news.

We then returned on a British ship to Seattle. From there I rode by bus to Bay City. At home, I was very disappointed to find that none of the photos I had taken turned out because of the cheap camera. I got to see Hopalong Cassidy on the British ship and asked where his horse was, to which he replied, "on the bottom deck where autos were parked." Hopalong gave me a dollar-sized silver token inscribed with the words, 'Good luck from Hoppy.' I have this token today, 71 years later.

One day, two girls in a car offered me a ride from Tillamook to Bay City. On the way to Bay City, I remember the driver (the best looking one of the two) saying, "There sure are a lot of woods around here. We are from Oregon City." I told the girls I had ONG drill that night, but if they came by the Tillamook Armory after drill we could go on a date and I would get my buddy to come also—his name was Bill Lane.

After our Thursday night training drill at 10 p.m. all the soldiers who smoked stood on the 30-foot-wide 9-foot-tall front steps and smoked. The two girls who I had lined up earlier drove by in a newer car, and all the men gave out with catcalls and whistles. The car stopped, Bill Lane and I got in, and we drove off. It was a great feeling to do this in front of all the other guys. We drove to Bay City so we could show the girls where we lived on Warren Street, one block away from each other. The girl who was driving drove to the end of the street at Tillamook Bay's edge and she parked in the exact same spot where my friend Jerry H. had transmission problems with his brother's car. We remained in the area for about two hours. We turned on the radio, opened the doors and the driver and I danced in the street before returning to the car's front seat where I lost my virginity. The girls drove Bill and me home, and we never heard from them again. On the way to our houses the girls admitted they ran away from home, were from Oregon City, and had taken their father's car without permission. I asked Bill if he had sex in the

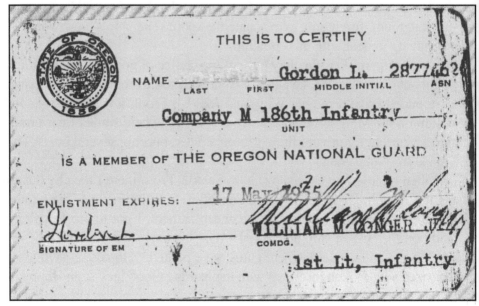

Gordon Lee's ONG ID Card.

ONG at North Fort Lewis Camp, Summer of 1952 ad 1953.

back seat and he said no, but after hearing the girls run away story Bill said he slipped a $5 bill in his girl's pocket without her noticing.

Upon arriving for duty my second summer at North Fort Lewis, CPL. Randy Witt, Company Clerk, who I worked with 40 hours a week, told me the Commanding Officer told him to promote me to PFC. Randy said he had more work than he could do so I had to report to the company office and type up my own promotion papers.

As our training was to be night training for 2 weeks, I hung out with CPL. Witt and helped him catch up on his duties. After dark, I would go with my squad into the woods littered with 3 to 6-foot ant hills and dig foxholes, command post holes, run communication wires, and other tasks. One highlight at the Fort was when our C.O. decided the motor pool sergeant's shirt was too dirty, so a full class A uniform inspection was held, and the sergeant was called to the front. They cut his shirt off of his back, a hole was dug, the shirt was buried as "Taps" was played, and there was a rifle salute using blank rounds.

On our first Friday in camp, we were told that 24-hour passes would be issued to soldiers in Class A uniforms. We lined up for our passes that took forever to be handed out. Soldiers referred to this as 'hurry up and wait.' We were then bussed to Downtown Tacoma. There were hundreds of soldiers on the streets with lots of MPs both walking and riding in Jeeps. The MPs stopped me and asked for my ID card and Liberty Pass. They also asked me to recite my serial number from memory for their enjoyment. Several prostitutes were also on the street. One enterprising girl about 20 years old held up her headscarf to the blowing wind and let it go calling out, "whoever gets my scarf gets me," which caused many soldiers to chase it down the street pushing and shoving each other. After this festivity, I returned to the pinball machine hall on the main drag. This was a building with 50 horse race machines spaced around the 4 walls. The machines didn't pay cash for games won, and cost 25 cents per game. There was a red light bulb above each machine that would light up at random once every hour. The business operator, who wore an apron with pockets full of quarters to make change for the customers, paid $25 cash to the person standing at the machine that the red light was on. The light bulb on the machine I sat down at lit up and the lady came over and handed me $25. She said, "you just got here, I should refuse to pay you."

I found what turned out to be my last summer job between school years. An ad in the Tillamook Newspaper read, 'Milker Wanted For 75 Cows. One-Bedroom House and Wages Depending on Experience.' I applied at the Teenie Ev-

The Circus Arcade

*The Luzon Building 1302-04 Pacific Avenue, Tacoma, WA. Circus Arcade
(1963). This was the arcade on the 'main drag' that Gordon Lee visited.
Image courtesy of the Tacoma Public Library (BU-14977).*

erman Dairy that was a half mile west of Tillamook on Bay Ocean Road. As I
had worked milking 25 cows on the Kilchis River farm, Teenie decided to hire
me for the rest of the summer months at $150 per month with a one-bedroom
house and meals provided at the main house.

On the Kilchis River farm, I used Surge milking machines and my new
job used DeLaval Milkers. We used 4 machines at one time due to the large
number of cows we had to milk. My job was about the same as on the Kilchis
River farm except that here I had to drive a flatbed truck and deliver the milk to
the Tillamook Cheese Factory 2 miles north on Highway 101 from Tillamook.
This job went smoothly and my summer vacation was soon over. It was time
for me to return to school and the 11th grade. It was hard to return home and
start school with my young, childish classmates after playing with the big boys.

Gordon Lee when he was 16 years old.

Gordon Lee - Starting forward 1952-1953.

11th Grade
1952-1953

One time, in the 11th grade, I was reading a school bulletin board, and a girl named Alice reached inside the back of my jeans and exclaimed out loud, "OH YOU HAVE NO SHORTS!" Another time in the school gym while seated on a bench I was told by a teacher, "You have no underwear on so cross your legs, I can see everything you have. Don't worry, I raised two boys and have seen it all before." I still wanted to crawl into a hole.

I felt I needed a bank savings account because of all the jobs I had, but I had saved nothing. I saw an ad bought by the Tillamook Commercial Bank that gave new customers a small savings coin bank. I went to the bank that was on Main Street near 3rd and received a bank book and small coin bank shaped like a book 4 inches long, 3 inches wide and a half inch thick with a coin slot in the top. The coin bank was locked and the bank teller told me to put coins in the small bank, bring it to the bank when it was full, then they would unlock it, and credit my savings account bank book with the deposit. This was a mandatory way to bank funds rather than spend the money.

In 1952, at age 16, I purchased an Ithaca brand, 12-gauge, double-barrel shotgun that was advertised for sale in the Tillamook Headlight Herald newspaper by a private party. The gun cost me $25 of the money I had earned working on the Dairy Farm. The gun had two problems—the gun stock was chipped, but I was able to fill it with wood dough. The second problem was if you pulled the left trigger, both barrels fired at the same time causing a lot of recoil. The right trigger worked fine. Rather than paying to have the left trigger repaired, I fired the right side first and made do.

To hunt ducks, the only requirement was an Oregon Hunting License. About one mile from our house, on Tillamook Bay, was a point of land extending about sixty feet out into the water at high tide, which was the only time duck hunting was productive.

There was a large log that had washed up onto the land point that I'd sit behind and conceal myself from the incoming flying ducks. I shot the ducks flying right over my head without them ever seeing me.

My favorite place to duck hunt was another half mile down the bay on the two ponds of saltwater that were about 100 feet wide and 300 feet long with 'No Trespassing' signs posted. This was one of the few places where green wing and blue wing teal ducks visited. The teal ducks did not feed on fish, so I thought they had a better flavor than those that did. A hunter could hear them coming before they saw them, because they made a sharp whistling noise. This was because of their slim head, body shape and the very fast pace they could fly. Most of the bay ducks fed on fish and had a slightly fishy taste. The best tasting ducks were wood ducks that lived on freshwater. I never shot a wood duck because they were so pretty with multi-colored feathers.

I also hunted in the flooded fields that were both north and south of Tillamook. Hunting the flooded fields required that you wore hip boots, as the water was two to three feet deep. I was able to shoot the most ducks in the field on the east side of Highway 101 about two blocks south of where the Tillamook Cheese Factory is now located. I always went duck hunting by myself. My family survived on wild game, fowl and fish, that we hunted and caught. Other than on Thanksgiving, I don't remember eating any kind of meat that was not shot or caught by us, except for hamburger in the summer after the deer and elk meat ran out.

Our family rarely ate seafood because my dad did not like the taste or smell of it. The only seafood that my dad would eat was oyster stew, which he cooked about two times per month on a Friday night.

As I was now 16 years old, I felt I could go into the local Tillamook Pool Hall. The hall had several pool tables. I played over 100 games of pool there and also played the 10-cent horse race pinball machine. If you were well informed you knew you could go to the bartender and he would come to the machine and remove the free games you had accrued and pay you 10 cents per game. I also used the cigarette machine by the front door to buy packs of cigarettes for 20 cents with 3 cents change sealed inside.

The way they kept track of what you owed for playing pool was the bartender came to your table and re-racked the balls when you alerted him your game was over by stamping the butt of your pool cue on the floor.

Players weren't allowed to rack up their own balls. The bartender collected 15 cents with each new re-rack. Tap Olympia Beer was sold at 10 cents per glass. They never asked me for ID. The club also had a card room.

At age 16, I dated D.M. (name withheld) who lived in Idaville, a mile South of my house, for 2 or 3 months. Her dad would try to embarrass her, just for fun, by asking me if I had any old socks because he didn't have any. One weekend, I helped him store a very ripe, stinking silage in the farm silo. I had to stand on the silage on the inside of the silo and arrange it with a pitchfork while it was being dumped into the silo from above.

I would pick up D.M. with my '41 Ford that I purchased for $300 to go on a date and then park in front of her house very late at night to talk and kiss. One night, D.M. got too excited and reached for my private parts and I pushed her hand away saying, "No." D.M. let out a yell and ran crying into her house. That was the end of our dates. In 1958, when my oldest son was born at the Tillamook Hospital, after the birth I walked into the 2-person recovery room and in the other bed was D.M. who had also just given birth. I never told my wife. I often wondered, what are the odds of that happening?

I took a job while in the 11th grade at Eastwood Shopping Center in Tillamook. I worked with a student from Tillamook High School named Gary Rush. We worked most weeknights and every Saturday. Our job was to stock shelves and to bag and/or carry out from one of the 4 check stands. This job was interesting but did not allow me time for after-school activities. A very heavy man shopped once per week and purchased two and sometimes three shopping carts full of groceries, sometimes spending over $100. The amount spent every week amazed me. Now I spend that much and am lucky to fill 3 bags, not the 20 to 30 bags he filled. A young man about 25 years old kept coming into the store to shop, and stop to talk. One time he told me he lived at the Tillamook Hotel and asked if I wanted to stop by after work and have a beer with him. I thought he was a good guy, so I said yes. I was only 17 at the time. After meeting him and having a beer, he said he and some friends were going to Seaside for the weekend and wanted to know if I would like to go. That's when I realized he was gay, then told him no and left. That was the first gay person I ever met. I felt guilty about drinking a beer at age 17, so I kept quiet.

Although I could buy all the beer I wanted in Tillamook County, it was next to impossible to buy hard liquor drinks in bars due to the strange Oregon Law for liquor sales. While I was growing up in Oregon, Liquor was only sold in state-owned liquor stores (only 4 or 5 were located in Tillamook County). It took strict I.D. to make a purchase if you looked to be under 25 years old. At age 15 I had purchased fake I.D. saying I was 21. The I.D. card cost me $5. I was afraid to use my fake I.D. in a state liquor store as I did not want to answer a lot of questions.

Bars in Oregon did not own any alcohol except for beer. Customers brought their own bottles of liquor into the bars they had purchased at the state-owned store. The bartender put their customer's bottle on the back bar with the owner's name on the bottle. When the customers ordered a drink, the alcohol came out of their own bottles. The bar charged a fee for use of their glassware, mixers, fruit for drinks, olives, onions, as well as for mixing and serving the drink. When leaving the bar, the customers were allowed to take their bottles of alcohol with them unless the bartender deemed them too intoxicated and held the bottle for 24 hours or until the customer was sober. Those customers who were afraid the bar might sell some of their stored alcohol put a mark on their bottle label, using a pen or their fingernail indicating what the contents level was when the bar took possession of the bottle per state law. Those persons not known to the bartender on duty had to show I.D. before they could purchase alcohol from stored bottles.

My dad had a bad toothache because, like our entire family, he didn't own a toothbrush or toothpaste. Dad had never been to a dentist and took care of toothaches himself. He went to his toolbox in the garage, found a pair of plyers and pulled out the rotten tooth. Later, when I was in the USMC in 1954, my mom took the bus to Portland by herself where she stayed a few days and had full dentures put in. I had full dentures by age 25.

While driving my 1941 Green Ford Convertible around Bay City with my girlfriend Shirley H., I would sit on the top of the seat and steer with my feet. Shirley would press on the gas to keep the car moving. This must have been a really strange sight to oncoming traffic. My car had loud twin tailpipes with a custom Porter muffler and a custom dial-a-tone on the lowered rear end. One young cop in Tillamook told me to keep my car out of Tillamook because of the loud noise it made. I had to park my car at the West end of town at A.F. Coats Lumber Company to avoid a ticket. I refused to remove my pipes.

Some Garibaldi High School boys who were on Bay City's rival sports team came to my house in Bay City and cut the top of my convertible. I had to take my car to a repair shop. Later, while in the USMC, Tommy L. confessed to me that he was one of the boys who cut my canvas car top.

My school year continued on with a new shop building class. Over the closed summer months, the school turned the room under the gym into a shop. I signed up for the new class and found I would spend an entire school year building my own house using plans and materials furnished by the school. This was an exciting class for me. Our houses were two stories high, 3 feet long and 2 feet wide. We were allowed to keep our houses at the end of the school year. My house was stored in my dad's garage for years. Our teacher (name withheld) got us started at the beginning of class every day for about 10 minutes and then left the class for the rest of the period, returning the last 5 minutes to see what progress we had made with our houses. After the teacher left, most of us crawled under the gym floor among the cobwebs to smoke.

I received an 'A' in the shop class and thought my house was a very good one. All of our 11th grade books that were furnished by the school had the usual notations written in them, like, "in case of fire throw this in" and Kilroy was here. (Insert graphic.)

I ordered a size 9 school ring made with 14k gold. It had the letters BCHS on it and my initials engraved inside the ring. When in the USMC and short of funds prior to payday, I would hock the ring for $25 cash and pay $30 to get it back. I loved my class ring. After I had returned from the USMC, my youngest brother asked me to loan him my ring because he wanted to give it to a girlfriend as a promise ring and he'd return it to me as soon as he could purchase another one. I never saw my ring again. When I asked my youngest brother for my ring back, he said he broke up with the girl and she refused to return the ring to him. Today I will pay $1,000.00 to anybody who returns my ring.

At the end of the school year (11th grade) in 1953, big changes were coming for high school students north of Tillamook through Nehalem. They built a new high school about one and a half miles north of Rockaway on Highway 101 called Neah-Kah-Nie High School. All high schools in the cities of Bay City, Garibaldi, Rockaway, Wheeler, and Nehalem would close and they would bus students to the new school. All grade schools would remain the same. There was a lot of negative talk about this new school, with the main concern being the wasted time spent on school buses and concern over bus accidents. My dad was all out against the new school policy, so when I told Mom and Dad I wasn't going to the new school it wasn't a problem.

After High School
1953

11th grade was over and I needed to plan on what to do during the summer other than the two weeks at North Fort Lewis. Joe H. and I decided to go to Banks, Oregon and work picking Bush Beans. We found a job and moved into a cabin in the work housing area provided to pickers at no charge. After less than two weeks, we were told that there were only two days remaining to pick. Rather than wait around that weekend, Joe H. and I quit. I told the owner of our plan and she got very mad and walked across the driveway, placing a padlock on our cabin door. We couldn't get our things, so we drove off in Joe's DeSoto. Joe wanted to return to Bay City, but I wanted our things in the locked cabin. I told Joe I planned on getting my possessions, so we made a plan. I returned to the work camp just before dark and knocked on the owner's door and asked her, "Is Joe here yet?" She said, "No. Why?" And I told her we returned to work the last two days for her. She smiled, thinking she had won. She handed me the key to unlock our cabin. I unlocked the padlock and packed all our things into boxes and Joe drove up in his DeSoto and we loaded it up and drove off. Now that bean season was over, we returned to Bay City to look for a summer job.

Joe went on to finish college at O.C.E. and got his certificate to teach school. He took a job with the State of Oregon as a parole officer in Salem and married a bartender who worked at Eola Inn just West of Salem. Joe talked me into getting a job at Oregon State Prison where I worked for nine years, making the rank of correctional sergeant. I knew Joe loved deer meat, and I had just shot one, so I took some deer steaks to Joe. One evening, I went to Joe's house in Salem to deliver the meat and his wife said Joe wasn't home and asked me if I wanted to go into the bedroom with her. I told her NO! I could not betray my family or my friend Joe. Joe got divorced, even though I never mentioned the incident about his wife to him, as I didn't want to hurt his feelings. Joe had one son who was about one-year-old at the time. I didn't hear from Joe again. Later I learned Joe quit his state job and moved to Seattle where he became an alcoholic and died alone in his room above a bar. I only wish I knew where my friend went. Maybe I could have helped him.

My friend, Gary Rush, suggested we both apply for a job at Tillamook County Cheese Factory. We applied and were both hired. I hitchhiked to and from work at the cheese factory. Going home from work, if I had worked with a cheese maker in the main vat room, I smelled like sour milk. People in the car I got a ride from looked at me funny so I'd have to explain the smell. Factory management found I was a fast learner and could do most jobs, so they classified me as a job fill-in worker, meaning I did any job where they were short-handed because of illness or other reasons. Sometimes I worked with the cheese maker at the vats making cheese curds from milk and then putting curds into various cans covered by cheesecloth, then putting them into a press where the curds were turned into solid loaves and wheels. The next day, I would dip large cheese wheels in wax coating, and on it went. They even assigned me to take tour groups into each work area. That doesn't happen today.

In October 1953, deer hunting season was about to open. Bob Ames, a guy about 40 years old, who I worked with at the Tillamook Cheese Factory, approached me about wanting to go hunting with me and my dad. Bob said he heard that my family were skilled hunters who always got our game animals and were known as 'wildlife outlaws.' I told Bob I would check with my dad to see if he could join us. My dad said it was okay if Bob followed our hunting rules. When told he could go with us, Bob was excited and asked what he should bring with him. I told him he should bring his rifle, binoculars, and good walking shoes, but not to bring a lunch as he could share ours, which was always two cans of pork and beans, two cans of corn beef and one loaf of white bread. We always had two sandwiches; one corn beef and one pork and beans on white bread. We usually only had creek water to drink. Bob was also told that we would leave our house in Bay City at 5 a.m. and we didn't wait for anyone running late.

The following Saturday, Bob showed up, ready to go hunting. Dad and I wanted to check his rifle and his binoculars. We were very surprised to find out Bob's rifle was an antique black powder single shot and his binoculars were nothing more than a plain glass toy. We did not comment about his equipment as we thought he was poor. We checked his hunting license and deer tag to ensure he had them. I told Bob to leave the kitchen knife he brought with him in his car because my dad and I had hunting knives on our belts.

All our family members had 270 Winchester rifles so we could use each other's ammunition if one of us was caught short on ammo. We also carried 7x50 binoculars as most of the deer and elk we found were spotted by using field glasses.

We were on our way on the first day of hunting season. We went to our favorite spot on the first day, called Felshaw Ridge, located in the Tillamook Burn. The ridge we intended to hunt was located up Kilchis River Road and on through God's Valley, continuing east about five miles on logging roads. We arrived at Felshaw Ridge just as the sun was coming up. We started our hunt, walking northbound on the top of the ridge, looking down both sides for deer. The first two deer we found were does, which we don't shoot. We always stay high on our hunts because deer and elk always run uphill to escape danger.

My dad was hunting on the east side of the ridge, and I had Bob hunting the west side of the ridge with me. Using my binoculars, I saw a 3-point deer about 500 yards downhill from us and had Bob look at the buck as I lay down behind a log so I could rest my rifle on it. Bob said, "you are not going to try to hit that deer at this distance, are you?"

I told Bob I would let him shoot it, but his gun wouldn't shoot that far. I aimed about 6" above the deer due to the distance I was shooting. I made an excellent shot, and the deer fell down dead. Bob said, "Wow."

We headed downhill to take care of and field dress the buck. My dad, who had heard my shot, came down the ridge to help with field dressing and carrying the meat out. We were able to drive within a half mile of the kill on a dirt cat road, so the pack out wasn't bad. We ate our lunch at our pickup and then continued our hunting trip until dusk, but we found no more buck deer that day. Bob said, while eating lunch, "This is the first time I have had a bean sandwich." We divided the meat up three ways after returning home.

I lost contact with Bob Ames when I joined the USMC in late October of that year. About ten years later, I ran into Bob, who was visiting Tillamook, and he told me why he had to hunt with an antique black powder gun. Bob said, at the time of our hunting trip, he was on parole for murder and could not own firearms. Bob said he found what he considered a loop-hole in the law that allows felons to own collectible antique fire arms. He thanked me for not asking any questions about his gun the day of our hunt-ing trip. I told Bob I had just thought he could not afford a newer rifle, and I didn't criticize poor people, because I've experienced that first-hand.

Another hunter who asked to go hunting with my family was a logger about 45 years old who was a friend of our family. Harry T. would not be a problem because of his hunting skills, and since he was a logger, he could get around in the Tillamook Burn without any problems. My dad and I decided on hunting north of Highway 6 up Jones Creek, which is about 15 miles East of Tillamook. We started our trip eastbound on Highway 6 and where the Wilson River first comes into view; I saw a very large 4-point buck deer swimming across the river, southbound, towards our pickup. On the far side of the river was a large dairy farm. We parked our pickup and ran towards the river as it was not lawful to shoot across a road. The deer kept coming and was now about 100 yards away. My dad took a shot and killed the four point. Dad didn't have much of a target because the only part of the deer that was above water was his head and antlers. Harry waded out about six feet into the river and pulled the buck ashore. Just as Harry used his knife and cut the buck's throat to bleed it out, a farmer came running, yelling, cussing, waving his arms, and shaking his fist. The deer must have hung out on the dairy farm and was considered a pet. We didn't know if the farmer had a gun or if he intended to come across the river. He was mad and acting like someone had just shot one of his kids. Harry handed me his rifle and lifted the deer on his back and ran up the hill to the pickup. Harry said he wished he had not cut the deer before he carried it to the car because the deer bled out on his back, soaking him. We drove about a mile up the road towards Jones Creek before we stopped at a turnout so Harry could take his calk boots off and wring out his socks. I wished I never saw the four point while I thought about how the dairy farmer must feel. It was a lawful taking of a big game animal, as landowners cannot own beaches or waterways in Oregon, but I still had a sad feeling.

We hunted the Jones Creek area the rest of the day but didn't get any more deer. I saw a full-grown cougar running across a canyon about 500 feet be-low me. The cougar's jumps were ten to fifteen feet long. I thought this was fitting because the Bay City High School Sports Teams were The Cougars. The team colors were purple and gold.

One day, I had the day off and decided to go to the Portland Zoo. I ran into a group of four guys I knew. Three had just graduated from Tillamook High School and one from Garibaldi. The guys told me they were in Portland to join the USMC. I decided, on the spot, to join the USMC with them. I had a good job at the cheese factory, but I was used to getting around with adventure.

I returned home and asked my mom to sign papers allowing me to join the Corps. A parent's signature was required for anyone under 18 years and I was only 17. Mom agreed to sign. The following day was a workday for me at the cheese factory. When I told my friend Gary Rush, who had worked with me at Eastwood Shopping Center and at the cheese factory he said, "I want to go with you." Gary was 18 years old. The next day, Gary and I went to the USMC Recruitment Office, where we found the other Tillamook County boys taking their physicals. A photographer from The Headlight Herald Newspaper arrived at the USMC recruitment office and took our picture, which went on the front page of the newspaper with a caption that read, 'Six Local Boys Join the U.S. Marine Corps'. I still have a copy of this photo.

Elden Hatfield, a Tillamook boy in our group, turned out to be my best friend in boot camp. Elden was also the best shooter in our platoon, and they kept him at the MCRD (Marine Corps Recruit Depot) as a rifle coach for other recruit platoons. My friend Gary Rush, who joined the Corps with me, became a hotel manager in Las Vegas after his tour of duty. My best friend in school, Jerry H., moved to Northern California to fall redwood trees and today he lives in Medford, Oregon. We still correspond and exchange holiday and birthday cards.

I purchased new clothes from a mail-order catalog as I had enough of Tillamook J. C. Penney Company's cheap junk. I needed the clothing for my trip to MCRD. I bought nice things, including my first pullover sweater and a pair of blue suede shoes that were just a little small for me, but I wore anyway. I did not know the USMC required that you have cash to mail your civilian clothing home, or you had to agree to donate your clothing. Due to my lack of funds, I had to donate my hard-earned, newly purchased clothing.

As I had prior service with the Oregon National Guard, they put me in charge of a group of boys going to MCRD from Portland. I held all the other boys' record files and air tickets to San Diego. They also gave me a quarter

Newspaper caption reads: Seven Tillamook county men Friday were sworn into the U.S. marine corps in Portland and shortly afterward departed for recruit training at San Diego, Cal. Gordon Lee is in the top row, second from the right. | Image Courtesy of The Headlight Herald.

Yellow Footprints

*If you can stand in these
yellow footprints
long enough,
you'll be tough enough
to earn the title of Marine,
forever.*

for a payphone and a phone number to call for transportation from the San Diego Airport. We went on a Western Air Line DC 12, a four-engine prop plane. Jet commercial aircraft was not in use yet.

Upon arrival at San Diego Airport, I wanted to make a good impression, being in charge and all, and was so excited when the MCRD answered the phone I said, "I have a group of men to be transported, we are at the Portland Airport, No, the San Diego Airport." The Marine Sergeant on the phone said, "Do you even know where the f*** you are?"

Soon after my conversation with the sergeant, a USMC 2 ½ ton truck arrived at the San Diego Airport to transport our group to Marine Corps Recruit Depot. We sat on the two benches in the back of the open-air truck bed. Upon arriving at the recruit depot, we passed through the main gate security checkpoint, manned by USMC MPs. After we arrived at our barracks, we were told to stand on the famous yellow footprints that were painted on the street that kept us all in one row maintaining the proper distance apart to await our drill instructor.

When all the yellow footprints were filled with new recruits, our drill instructor walked out of the barracks, looked up and down the line, and said, "I am your drill instructor [name withheld]. You had better give your soul to God because your a** belongs to me."

He then pointed to the biggest recruit in the line and said, "You fat boy, get your fat butt up here." The person called up front was of Asian descent, about 20 years old, 6'4" and just over 300 lbs. The recruit went forward to stand in front of the DI and the DI asked him, "What in the hell are you?!" The recruit replied, "I'm Private Wong, sir, a Marine." The DI reached out and hit him on the chin, knocking him unconscious onto the street. The DI stepped over the body and pointed at us yelling, "You f***ing people are not Marines until I say you are Marines!"

Standing there, I reflected on the fact that I was no longer living a quieter, more peaceful life in Bay City, Oregon. I was now living a more exciting life in the U.S. Marine Corps. But that's another story.

The biggest reward for writing a book about my life are the memories brought back, some of which I have not thought about in several years and being able to share them with others.

As far as this book goes, this is THE END. But life goes on . . .

My Occupations
After Growing Up In Bay City

Army National Guard – PFC (2 years)

USMC – Sergeant (3 years)

Diamond Lumber Company – Dry End Supervisor (5 years)

Oregon State Prison – Sergeant (9 years)

City Police (Over 20 years)

First Sergeant, Salem PD Reserve (8 years)

Motorcycle Officer, La Grande (1 year)

McMinnville Patrol Officer (5 years)

Cornelius Police Sergeant (5 years)

Detective Sergeant (5 years)

Washington County Major Crime Team Detective Sergeant (2 years)

Chief of Police (1 year)

Traveling Coin Dealer (10 years)

Sports Card Store Owner (3 years)

Antique Dealer (24 years)

While employed at Oregon State Prison, I missed a total of 4 hours of work for any reason, and it was when I had all my lower teeth pulled. I went back to work 4 hours after my dental appointment.

I was able to work the remaining 4 hours of my shift because I was the Administrative Assistant to the Captain and had my own office so I could spit blood in a coffee cup.

In 1960, while working swing shift (4 p.m. to midnight) on a green chain pulling wood off and stacking it, at Diamond Lumber Company, I had all my upper teeth pulled. The doctor was only 5' tall and 100 lbs. He had to stand on a wood box to reach my mouth. He could not budge my eye teeth so he screwed a clamp on them and hit the clamp with a hammer with his wife holding my head upright, using a folded towel across my forehead and pulling from behind me. I went to work that same day at 4 p.m., pulled and stacked lumber and spit blood for 8 hours so I could feed my family. Mill-work was NO WORK, NO PAY. In my life, I've worked 68 years for wages and only taken those 4 hours off from work.

KILROY WAS HERE

Recap of Moneymaking Ventures

4th Grade - 11th Grade

Portland, Oregon

Delivered Shopping News
Sold cherries door to door
Sold produce door to door
Age 10 - Cleaned elderly person's home
Held a Carnival for other kids

Bay City, Oregon

Picked wild foxglove plants 5 cents per lb.
Picked wild blackberries 5 cents per lb.
Peeled Cascara Bark 7 cents wet – 21 cents dry
Picked up bottles along Highway 101 for refunds
5th grade - Hunted Golf Balls to sell for 6 years at Alderbrook Golf Course
6th grade - Took care of Neighbor's rabbits 1 month
7th grade - Did yardwork with a landscaper
After 8th -grade - Picked strawberries at Gales Creek
After 8th grade - Worked over 2 months on Kilchis River Farm
After 9th grade - Picked Cherries at Salem, Oregon
10th grade – Pinsetter at Tillamook Bowling Alley
10th grade – Delivered Oregonian Newspaper 1 year
10th grade - Joined the Oregon National Guard with pay
10th grade – Worked full time at ONG Armory
10th grade - Worked over 2 months on Everman Dairy
11th grade - Worked at Eastwood Shopping Center as a stock boy
After 11th grade - Picked Bush Beans at Banks, Oregon
After 11th grade - Tillamook Cheese Factory Employee

Author's
Literary Background

1971
Field and Stream Magazine Award for, "A Tillamook Burn Deer Hunt," article.

1979
Awarded the Dr. Conway Bolt Literary Award at the Middle Atlantic Numismatic Association Convention on 11-25-79 for Best Articles for the Year 1979.

1979
Voted for a cash prize and trophy by membership for Best Articles Written for The Mana Monthly Journals.

1980
Author of "The Sport of Queens" – A book about dog race betting using progressive and regressive wagers. The betting system is proven by annual pay facts for win-pace-show for three consecutive years in Portland, Oregon. (This book is out of print). Dated 1978.

1981
Featured Columnist for the Journals of "The Numismatic Association of Southern California," a monthly publication.

January 1983
Author of "Oregon Town Trade Tokens," "Washington State Town Trade Tokens," and "Nevada Town Trade Tokens."

1979 Dr. Conway Bolt Literary Award

1971 Field and Stream Award.

1985
A Listing of Thirty Nevada Counterfeit Merchant Trademark Tokens at Tonopah, Nevada.

1986
Lumber Token Article Published in the ATCO, "Active Token Collectors Organization" a Sioux Falls, South Dakota Journal.

Books In The Works

Fun Things To Do Along Tillamook Bay

Buying and Selling Antiques and Collectibles

Doing Time: Nine Years in a State Prison

Police Command Sergeant: 8101 is 10-7 at My X:
Twenty Years of Memories While Working as a Police Officer

The manuscripts for these books are already completed and awaiting
publication. All titles are subject to change.

Oregon State Tuberculosis Hospital in Salem, Oregon.

After Bay City

Police

As a police sergeant, they assigned me to the security detail for New York governor Nelson Rockefeller and his wife, "Happy" Rockefeller when he campaigned for U.S. President. I walked with, talked with, and was invited by him to stop by his office any time without an appointment. I was also on a security detail for governor Mark Hatfield. I met several other political people including JFK.

I was on the security detail or served as a bodyguard for over three dozen celebrities including Johnny Cash, June Carter, Doris Day, Boxcar Willy, Willie Nelson and more. I have many autographs and photos of myself with celebrities.

State Prison

I transported Oregon State Prisoners who had TB to the TB hospital. In Oregon, they required persons with active TB to be locked up and treated. I also transported inmates who were mentally ill to the Oregon state mental hospital and those returning to the prison after treatment. Our prison inmates were placed on ward #38, Maximum Security. This was the same mental hospital that was filmed in the movie One Flew Over the Cuckoo's Nest. I transported several mentally ill inmates: one that ate bugs, one that took off his clothing in the recreation yard on days that it rained and dove off the top of the grandstand into mud puddles, those who cut themselves bad, (one I escorted required 132 stitches and was in an upper body cast due to eating his arm) and those inmates who cut officers with homemade shanks. Two of my fellow officer friends were killed with homemade knives while standing the line (a red line inmates walked, single file, while search officers searched every 1 in 10 inmates or so as they passed by). My friends, officer Al Schmidt and Sgt. Robert Geer were killed on the line I had stood beside several hundred times while searching inmates.

A friend holding the rank of lieutenant was being held in C block during the 1968 riot. They lowered me and another sergeant over the 34-foot wall at 2 a.m. with a hacksaw and we used it to cut the bars on the cell house window to free the lieutenant. The three of us were then pulled up the wall with ropes to make our escape.

In D cell block, rioting inmates on all five tiers refused to return to their cells. We trained a 3-inch fire hose on them and convinced them to enter their cells to avoid being washed down the tier's catwalks.

Reno

I lived in Reno, Nevada for three years during the 1980s and was a professional black jack gambler. During this time, I also bought and sold antiques and collectibles, which were mostly western items such as bits, saddles, and other memorabilia. The casino pit bosses are pretty smart and can spot a professional gambler. When you are "found out," The pit boss stands right in front of your table space, writes down your wins or losses, asks if you want a chip box (this makes their job easier because they can tell at a glance how many of the house chips you have), and otherwise harass you in hopes you will leave. One casino had me escorted to the door, where I was told to go away and win someone else's money.

Travel

I have done a lot of travel going to Mexico over a dozen times, to Canada two times, to Europe four times (one time for 60 days and three times for 30 days). I have visited most U.S. states, Africa and every country in Europe except five, due to the danger of 'unrest' as advised by our government.

I was held up in Budapest, Hungary by two girls on the city street at midnight, one of which was holding a 45 automatic handgun 3 inches from my face. I was asked for my passport, cash and gold neck chain. I refused to give them anything, turned my back to them and walked away while closing my eyes thinking I would be shot in the back. The girls did not shoot me and I walked to my hotel room.

I paid 300 West German Marks to visit East Berlin before the wall came down. We boarded a bus at Checkpoint Charlie in West Berlin for our supervised tour of East Berlin. There were three Russian officers in dress uniforms aboard the bus. They drove us through the East Berlin business district that had no lights on and all the buildings were drab as none had been painted in 49 years. Department store windows were empty. A grocery store had a line of shoppers on the sidewalk. The Russian guide explained only five shoppers were allowed inside the store and when one came out of the store another shopper could go in. They drove us to an East German Museum and to a World War II Russian cemetery. I was looking forward to having an East German lunch to see what their food was like. I told a food server the food looked the same as West German food and she said, "It is West German food. We bring it here just for you." The server also said, "There are no restaurants open in East Berlin." I gave the server a West German 5 Mark tip, and she thought she had died and gone to heaven. The West German mark was worth several times the value of East German money. I took a chance giving the East German food server some money. I gave her the banknote when the Russian guards were not looking. A few months later I returned to Berlin because the Berlin wall was coming down. I brought a hammer and a chisel and banged on the wall. I was able to knock off about 20 one-inch wide and one-inch-high chunks of the wall. I gave away some of the wall chunks as gifts, kept some for myself and sold the rest for $25 each in my collectible store. I had a German lady take my picture, with my camera at the wall, with me holding my hammer and chisel so I had proof that the Berlin wall chunks were real.

My greatest accomplishment was to make peace with my dad before his passing in October 2003, at 90 years of age. In 1989, I purchased a new 3/4 ton Chevrolet van that Dad and I used for many trips. Our trips lasted from 1 to 3 weeks each and we traveled to about two-thirds of the states, Mexico and Canada. We planned a trip every other month for 13 years, putting 250,000 miles on my van. We visited L.A., Las Vegas, Tombstone, Dallas, Nashville, Branson, Missouri and Nebraska where we stayed at Uncle Lee's home, visited our relation, went to Omaha and took Uncle Lee with us to visit our farm where we grew up in Creighton, Nebraska. Dad and I split the bills for gas and food and shared motel rooms.

Memorable Life Experiences

At Age 15, drove a 2 ½ ton Army truck to an Army camp in Portland to pick up supplies for the National Guard Armory in Tillamook, Oregon every 3 months for a year.

At Age 19, was a UMSC sergeant troop handler and close order drill sergeant while stationed in Hawaii 1 ½ years.

At Age 26, supervised 13 employees at Diamond Plywood Co. at the Blimp Base in Tillamook, Oregon.

Gained the rank of sergeant while employed at the Oregon State Prison, where he worked nine years.

Was the store security officer and store detective at Meier and Frank Department Store in Salem, Oregon every Friday night and all day on Saturdays for three years during his off-duty hours at Oregon State Prison.

Oregon State Prison vehicle driver for Warden C.T. Gladden.

Went out of state to return escaped prisoners using prison vehicles and/or airlines. Returned between 40 and 50 inmates to the prison.

Supervised a 21-inmate tree planting crew. These inmates also worked at Silver Falls State Park, making trails.

Supervised a 51-man inmate fire-fighting crew at a forest fire at The Dalles, Oregon and also near La Grande, Oregon. Supervisor 24 hours per day.

Supervised all death row visits for seven years. He was also the person used for practice runs prior to an execution and was executed while strapped in the gas chamber chair 4 times by Warden Gladden then carried out, placed on the lawn and hosed off with a fire hose to rid his body of fake gas. He was then placed in a hearse and taken to Oregon State Hospital Morgue. This gave his mother nightmares.

Served during the riot at Oregon State Prison for 18 months on the prison riot squad working 16 hours per day assigned to gas gun operator.

During the riot, he carried a footlocker filled with sandwiches and a milk can full of coffee from the administration building to the prison recreation yard with one other officer. The inmate heading up the riot said the rioting inmates would feed the seven prison staff members held hostage on the yard if the prison staff fed the convicts. They were also guaranteed safety. All the fire alarms sounded and the prison industries sprinklers were going off causing 3 inches of water on the avenue leading to the yard. They had to step over bodies lying on the blacktop because the rioting inmates had destroyed the prison hospital and had stolen and used the drugs. Prison officers and state police were on building tops and the prison wall with automatic rifles watching their every move.

Worked with Federal Marshals escorting State Prison inmates to jail cells in the federal courthouse in Portland, Oregon.

Went on several manhunts when inmates escaped from the prison farm and/or the prison forest camp near Tillamook. Two officers per prison car were equipped with radios and two 30-30 rifles.

Was a uniform police sergeant while supervising all home games for the AAA Salem Dodger baseball team for one year.

Was a uniform police sergeant while working extra hours at the Oregon State Fair as a security officer for seven seasons.

Was a motorcycle officer at La Grande, Oregon. Shot a vicious dog (black lab) through the head that had bitten a young boy and was in mid-air going for his Sergeant's neck. The dog fell dead at his feet. He had told the Sergeant he would cover him while he tried to net the dog, and he did.

Started and supervised (on his own time) two youth police cadet programs. One group had 11 boys and in another city the group had 24 boys and 2 girls. These groups were funded by donations and money earned by the cadets.

Shot one fleeing felon near a car dealership.

Saved at least four lives while employed as a police officer. One life saved was that of a young boy about 2 years old who wasn't properly supervised and left his yard and wandered on the railroad tracks near his home, fell and hit his head and was unconscious and laying between the railroad tracks. A second life was that of a 10-year-old boy who had reached through a broken plate-glass window which fell down on his arm when he bumped it. The boy's arm was cut to the bone. He just happened to see both boys while driving by. He also saved a lady he found in a ditch full of water, under her wrecked Volkswagen car. She was having trouble keeping her head above water while pinned by her car. He took off his gun belt and boots and went into the water and placed her head on his legs to keep her above water until a wrecker arrived to lift the car off of her. The fourth life he saved was that of a young man whose brains he held and pushed back into his head after an accident. He used the injured man's shirt to press on his head to stop the bleeding until Life Flight arrived. The shirt of the young man was used to avoid infection. (Note: just checking was it your shirt or HIS shirt?) The one-car accident happened about 3 minutes before he arrived on scene. This person is grateful for my actions and is alive and well today. He likely saved many more lives during his 20 years of duty as a policeman, but these are the most memorable.

Made several drug arrests as a detective sergeant on the Major Crime Team (2 years).

Made two arrests for Murder 1 during a 3-week period while working as a city police Sgt. detective, homicide. The most difficult cases he investigated were that of a female with no head and a male who had been dead for over two months, found lying on his bathroom floor during the summer months.

Once while in pursuit of a theft suspect, he hit a female deer with a patrol car while traveling over 130 mph. The deer slammed into his front bumper and went clear to the vehicle firewall. His vehicle was a total wreck, but he wasn't injured.

Peeling Cascara Bark

Cascara Trees are found throughout Tillamook County mixed in with vine maple and Alder. The trees' bark is removed from Cascara tree trunks using a knife, and a gunny sack is used to carry the bark in. Sometimes the tree limbs are also peeled if they are big enough. The underside of the removed bark is bright yellow when cut off. The bare tree trunk is also bright yellow and is very slick due to lots of sticky sap. The bark comes off fast. A 20-foot tree can be peeled in 10 minutes.

Cascara bark was used by Native Americans and was called Chittum. Buyers paid 7 cents per lb. wet and 21 cents per lb. if dried. The bark lost about half the weight if dried, so there was not much to gain by drying it.

Cascara bark is used as a laxative. If you were a child and didn't drive, peeling bark was a hard way to earn money. First, you had to walk 3 to 5 miles to locate the bark, peel it and then walk another 3 to 5 miles with 40 to 50 lbs. of bark on your back, to deliver it to the buyer.

Picking Fox Glove

Fox Glove is a plant with broad leaves that grows 6 inches to 18 inches tall. Some plants have white bell-like flowers and some plants have purple flowers. In late summer, flowers turn to seed. To pick foxglove you need a very sharp knife and a gunny sack. The entire plant is cut off near the ground and flowers discarded. Buyers paid 7 cents per lb. for the green plants. Foxglove grows in direct sunshine and loves clay or fresh dirt logging cat roads. I never gathered the dry seed in late fall, but those who did were paid $1.45 per lb. Each plant has many seeds but they are very tiny and I think it would take over 400 seeds to make a pound. To harvest the seed, the plants were shook causing the seeds to fall onto a cloth placed under the plant. The foxglove plant is used to make a heart medication called Digitalis. A gunny sack full of foxglove will weigh 50 to 60 lbs.

Please Review This Book

If you enjoyed this book, please leave a review on Amazon, Goodreads, or wherever books are sold. We greatly appreciate your feedback! Thank you for purchasing a book from an indie publisher and indie author!

Join Gordon Lee's List

Find out about upcoming releases, his latest author news, special promotions, and other reader opportunities by joining Lee's e-mail list. He will never sell or share your information. To subscribe, go to the link below or click the QR code:

https://caliber-press.com/gordonlee/author-news/

Follow Gordon Lee on Instagram: @authorgordonlee
Follow Gordon Lee on Twitter: @authorgordonlee
Like Gordon Lee on Facebook: facebook.com/AuthorGordonLee

Join the Caliber Press List

Find out about upcoming releases, press news, special promotions, and other reader opportunities by joining our e-mail list. We will never sell or share your information. To subscribe, go to the link below or click the QR code:

https://caliber-press.com/newsletter/

Follow Caliber Press on Instagram: @caliberpress
Follow Caliber Press on Twitter: @caliberpress
Like Caliber Press on Facebook: facebook.com/caliberpress

Made in United States
Troutdale, OR
11/27/2023

15026257R00094